Editor
Heather Douglas

Managing Editor
Karen J. Goldfluss, M.S. Ed.

Illustrator
Howard Cheney

Cover Artist
Brenda DiAntonis

Creative Director
Karen J. Goldfluss, M.S. Ed.

Art Production Manager
Kevin Barnes

Art Coordinator
Renée Christine Yates

Imaging
Denise Thomas
James Edward Grace
Nathan Rivera

Publisher
Mary D. Smith, M.S. Ed.

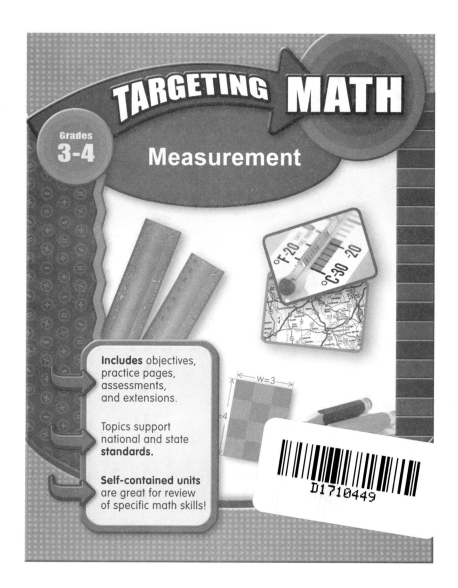

TARGETING MATH

Grades 3-4

Measurement

Includes objectives, practice pages, assessments, and extensions.

Topics support national and state **standards**.

Self-contained units are great for review of specific math skills!

D1710449

Authors

Jo Grinham, Judi Tertini, and Angela Toohey

(Revised and rewritten by Teacher Created Resources, Inc.)

Teacher Created Resources, Inc.
6421 Industry Way
Westminster, CA 92683
www.teachercreated.com
ISBN-13: 978-1-4206-8992-1
© 2007 Teacher Created Resources, Inc.
Made in U.S.A.

Teacher Created Resources

Table of Contents

Table of Contents

Introduction

Targeting Math

The series Targeting Math is a comprehensive resource for elementary schools. It has been developed so that teachers can find activities and reproducible pages for all areas of the elementary math curriculum.

About This Series

The twelve books in the series cover all aspects of the math curriculum in an easy to read format. Each level - grades 1 and 2, grades 3 and 4, and grades 5 and 6 - has four books: Numeration and Fractions; Operations and Number Patterns; Space and Chance and Data; and Measurement. Each topic in a book is covered by one or more units that are progressive in level. You are able to find resources for all your students whatever their ability. This enables you to differentiate for different ability groups, within your class. It also allows you to quickly find worksheets at different levels for remediation and extension.

About This Book

Targeting Math: Measurement (Grades 3 and 4) contains the following topics: Length; Area; Mass, Volume and Capacity, Angles, and Time. Length contains three units, Area, Mass, Volume and Capacity, and Time contain two units, and Angles contains one unit. (See Table of Contents for specific skills.)

About Each Unit

Each unit is complete in itself. It begins with a list of objectives, resources needed, mathematical language used, and a description of each reproducible. This is followed by suggested student activities to reinforce learning. The reproducible pages cover different aspects of the topic in a progressive nature and all answers are included. Every unit includes an assessment page. Each assessment page is an important resource in itself as teachers can use each one to find out what their students know about a new topic. They can also be used for assessing specific objectives when clear feedback is needed.

About the Skills Index

A Skills Index is provided at the end of the book. It lists specific objectives for the student pages of each unit in the book.

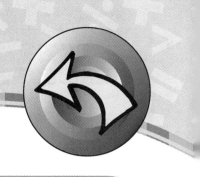

LENGTH

There are three units relating to length.

Students are encouraged to demonstrate an understanding of length through activities based on perimeter, measuring and recording distances. Lengths are ordered and measurements converted to larger or smaller units.

The skills of estimating and checking calculations are encouraged.

There is some calculator work and there are problem-solving exercises involving everyday situations. Correct use of a ruler is practiced in measuring lines and drawing lines to a given length.

There are three assessment pages and two activity pages.

ESTIMATING AND CALCULATING LENGTH

Unit 1

**Estimating
Measuring
Perimeter
Inch
Ordering length**

Objectives

- measures perimeter
- uses standard and informal units
- tests estimates of physical quantities using appropriate informal units
- estimates, measures, and records the length of objects in inches
- sorts and describes objects in terms of their features such as size
- estimates, compares, orders, and measures the length of objects and the distance between objects using informal units
- uses available technology to help in the solution of mathematical problems
- uses number skills involving whole numbers to solve problems

Language

estimate, long, perimeter, lengths, nearest, inch, actual, height, tallest, shortest, distances, biggest, longest, lap, smallest, check

Materials/Resources

Base 10 materials (unit cubes or centicubes), ruler, colored pencils, calculator, geoboard, rubber bands, string

Contents of Student Pages

* Materials needed for each reproducible student page

Page 8 Measuring Length
Using a ruler to measure – inches
* colored pencils, ruler

Page 9 Heights
Matching heights – match models to written descriptions.
* colored pencils, unit cubes

Page 10 Using Length with Perimeter
Geoboard shapes – smallest/largest perimeters; making shapes of a given perimeter; finding perimeters.
* geoboards, colored pencils, rubber bands

Page 11 Perimeter
Estimating and measuring perimeter; measuring lines.
* calculator, ruler

Page 12 Assessment
* ruler

Page 13 Activity Page—Slug Trails
Measuring the lengths of different slug trails.

. . . .
Remember

- ❏ As estimation plays a vital role in the development of understanding, provide many opportunities for students to estimate.
- ❏ Give students as many opportunities as possible to measure.
- ❏ Integrate measuring activities into other key learning areas.

Additional Activities

- ❏ Read "Jack and the Beanstalk" to the students – integrate with Visual Arts and make a wall display of the story.
- ❏ Allow students opportunities to make simple finger puppets and to attach legs (streamers) of various lengths.
- ❏ Provide opportunities for students to have many experiences in the use of calipers and rulers and tape measures.
- ❏ As a class, make charts, "Things that are 1in., 1/2 in., 1/4 in., 12 in." in length. Add to it regularly when a discovery is made.
- ❏ As a class discuss how people used to measure using digits, cubits, palm, span, etc. Allow students to measure objects using these measurements. Discuss use with students.
- ❏ What is it like to be very short or very tall? Provide opportunities for students to experience things if they were short (get down on knees); if they were tall (stand on tables etc.). Discuss advantages and disadvantages.
- ❏ In visual arts, divide students into groups and allow them to choose and make something a foot or yard long. Put on display.
- ❏ Don't forget to go into the playground and give students opportunities to measure objects.

Answers

Page 8 Measuring Length
1. a. 3 ½ in.
   b. 5 in.
   c. 5 ½ in.
   d. 6 in.
2. Teacher to check.

Page 9 Heights
1. a. From left to right: Robert, Paul, Kelly, Peter, Linn Linn, Madge
   b. Teacher to check.

Page 10 Using Length with Perimeter
1. Teacher to check.
2. a. 24
   b. 18
   c. 12
   d. 32

Page 11 Perimeter
1. a. 6 in.
   b. 4 in.
   c. 6 in.
2. a. 50 in.
   b. 142 in.
   c. 82 in.
3. a. 4 ½ in.
   b. 3 in.
   c. 1 ½ in.
   d. 4 in.

Page 12 Assessment
1. a. 2 ½ in.
   b. 3 in.
   c. 3 ½ in.
   d. 1 in.
   e. 5 ½ in.
2. a. 22 in.
   b. 18 in.
   c. 22 in.
   d. 32 in.
   e. 12 in.
   f. 30 in.
3. Teacher to check.

Page 13 Activity Page—Slug Trails
1. a. Sal
   b. 9 ½ ft.
   c. 1 in.
2. 4 nights

Name	Date

1. Use a ruler to measure the length of these buses to the nearest half inch. Estimate first.

a.

Estimate

Actual

b.

Estimate

Actual

c.

Estimate

Actual

d.

Estimate

Actual

2. Color: the 5 in. bus red, the 6 in. bus blue, the 5 ½ in. bus yellow, the 3 ½ in. bus orange.

8

Name   **Date**

You need unit cubes and colored pencils.

1. Here are the heights of some people. Look at the chart and then name the people.
   Color the people.

> Kelly – 68 in., basketball player.
>
> Robert – 107 in., tallest man in the world.
>
> Linn Linn – 39 in.
>
> Madge – 26 in., shortest living woman in the world.
>
> Paul – 81 in., football player.
>
> Peter – 59 in., student.

b. Turn over the page and draw Robert's hand. It was 29 unit cubes long.

_____ _____ _____

_____ _____ _____

⑨

Name	**Date**

You need colored pencils, a geoboard and rubber bands.

1. **a.** Make some shapes on the geoboard. Which one has the biggest perimeter? Draw it here with a red pencil.

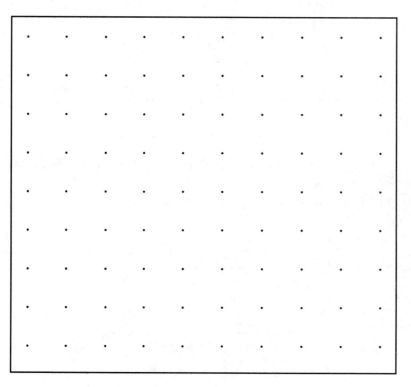

   b. Draw the shape with the smallest perimeter using a blue pencil.

   c. Using a green pencil, draw a shape with a perimeter of 10 units.

   d. Using a yellow pencil, draw a shape with a perimeter of 20 units.

2. Make each shape on your geoboard and then find its perimeter.

   a. 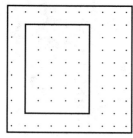 **b.** 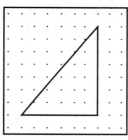 **c.** 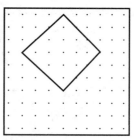 **d.**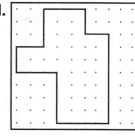

   P = _____   P = _____   P = _____   P = _____

Name	**Date**

1. Estimate and then use a ruler to find the perimeters.

   a.   **b.**   **c.**

   Estimate _____ in.   Estimate _____ in.   Estimate _____ in.

   Actual P = _____ in.   Actual P = _____ in.   Actual P = _____ in.

2. Find the perimeter of these towels. Use a calculator to check.

   a.   **b.**   45 in.   **c.**

   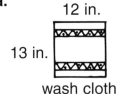   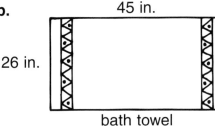   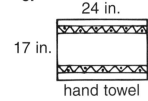

   wash cloth   bath towel   hand towel

   P = _____ in.   P = _____ in.   P = _____ in.

3. Measure the length of each line using a ruler. Estimate first.

   a. _____ Estimate   Actual

   b. _____ Estimate   Actual

   c. _____ Estimate   Actual

   d. _____ Estimate   Actual

Name	**Date**

1. Find the length of these pencils to the nearest inch.

a.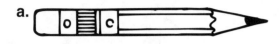

b.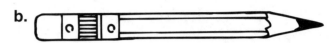

_____ in.   _____ in.

c.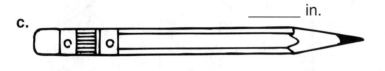

d.

_____ in.   _____ in.

e.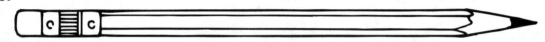

_____ in.

2. Find the perimeter of these rectangles.

a.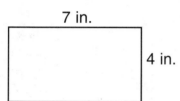

7 in. / 4 in.

P = _____ in.

b.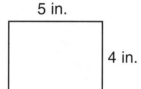

5 in. / 4 in.

P = _____ in.

c.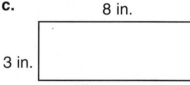

8 in. / 3 in.

P = _____ in.

d.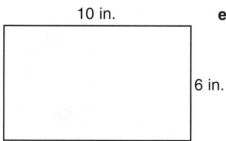

10 in. / 6 in.

P = _____ in.

e.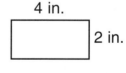

4 in. / 2 in.

P = _____ in.

f.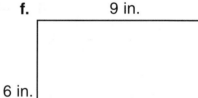

9 in. / 6 in.

P = _____ in.

3. Draw lines of:

  a. 2 ½ in.

  b. 4 in.

  c. 5 in.

(12)

Name	**Date**

Measure Each Slug Trail

1. Use a piece of string to find out which slug travels the furthest to find its lunch.

   a. Who traveled the furthest? _____

   b. If 1in. = 1 foot how far did Sam travel? _____

   c. What is the difference between Sid's trail and Sue's trail? _____

2. Sid Snail is at the bottom of the compost heap. The compost heap is 36 inches deep and Sid wants to reach the top for some fresh air. Each night he crawls up 10 in. but while he is asleep he slips back 4 in. How many nights crawling will it take for Sid to reach the top of the compost heap?

13

LENGTH, WIDTH, AND PERIMETER

Unit 2

**Estimating
Perimeter
Length and Differences
Ordering
Problem solving**

Objectives

- *measures perimeter*
- *directly and indirectly compares length*
- *checks, using an alternative method if necessary, whether answers to problems are correct and sensible*
- *uses number skills involving whole numbers to solve problems*
- *estimates and measures the length of objects in inches and feet*
- *uses one or more strategies to solve mathematical problems*
- *poses questions or problems about mathematical situations*
- *estimates, compares, orders and measures the length of objects and distances between objects using informal units*

Language

height, shortest, tallest, order, how much taller, how much wider, width, biggest, perimeter, length, longer side, altogether

Materials/Resources

scissors, glue, colored pencils, scratch paper, calculator, ruler, dice, counters

Contents of Student Pages

* *Materials needed for each reproducible student page*

Page 16 Heights
Reading a table of heights – answer questions using given information.

Page 17 Width
Comparing widths – using an advertisement; drawing given width.
* *paper, ruler and colored pencils*

Page 18 Drawing Length
Finding lengths of longer sides of rectangles by measuring.
* *rulers*

Page 19 Length Problems
Solving length problems – make up your own length problem

Page 20 Perimeter
Decide on suitable length; find new measurements; find perimeters.
* *calculators*

Page 21 Assessment
Page 22 Activity Page—Make the Change
Game – converting large measurements to smaller measurements.
* *dice, calculators*

Remember

- ❑ *Give students many opportunities to measure.*
- ❑ *Reference material in books, computer programs and CD ROMs provide material that can be used in the length unit.*

14

Additional Activities

❏ *Read to the students* The BFG *by Roald Dahl and integrate with visual arts. Make the BFG and some of his belongings.*

❏ *Research the world record for the long jump. Measure in a long jump pit and then see how far students can jump.*

❏ *Encourage students to bring catalogs from home that show length measurement, (e.g. televisions). Discuss and make into a wall chart.*

❏ *Give students opportunities to use paper, scissors, glue, etc. to create real-size objects. Students can guess perimeters and then measure.*

❏ *Measure everyone in the class in inches. Order from shortest to tallest. As a class, find differences in height.*

❏ *Bring towels of different sizes into the classroom and allow students to measure them.*

❏ *Encourage students to measure objects at home. Discuss as a class and record, (e.g. largest perimeter of a book, length of a ball).*

❏ *Integrate measuring into other key learning areas.*

Answers

Page 16 Heights
1. a. number 10
   b. number 1
   c. numbers 19, 4, 15, 34, 1
   d. number 14
   e. number 32
   f. 1 in.
   g. 12 in.
   h. 10, 5, 14, 11, 2, 32, 23, 19, 34, 4, 15, 1
   i. 1 in.
2. 1 and 10

Page 17 Width
1. From smallest to largest: 13 in., 19 in., 20 in., 23 in., 27 in., 31 in., 41 in., 51 in.
2. a. 7 in.
   b. 6 in.
   c. 4 in.
   d. 7 in.
   e. 10in.
3. Teacher to check.

Page 18 Drawing Length
1. Teacher to check.
2. a. 10 in.
   b. 6 in.
   c. 18 in.
   d. 11in.

Page 19 Length Problems
1. a. 8 yd.
   b. 27 yd.
   c. 2 ft.
   d. 2 ft.
   e. 3 ft.
   f. 14 yd.
   g. 12 yd.
2. Teacher to check.

Page 20 Perimeter
1. Teacher to check.
2. a. 297 in.
   b. 237 in.
   c. 177 in.
   d. 117 in.
3. a. 800 in.
   b. 800 in.
   c. 796 in.
   d. 580 in.
   e. 564 in.
   f. 574 in.

Page 21 Assessment
1. a. false
   b. true
2. a. 49 in.
   b. 187 in.
3. Teacher to check.
4. a. 12 in.
   b. 16 in.
   c. 23 in.
   d. 24 in.
5. a. 12 in.
   b. 6 in.
   c. 9 in.
6. a. 4 in.
   b. 43 yd.
   c. 250 yd.

Name	Date

1. Here is a table of the heights of some of the Mighty Tigers football team.

Number	Height
4 . . . . .75 in.	
15 . . . . .78 in.	
2 .71 in.	
23 . . . . .72 in.	
34 . . . . .74 in.	
1 .80 in.	

Number	Height
11 .70 in.	
32 .71 in.	
19 .73 in.	
14 .70 in.	
10 .68 in.	
5 .69 in.	

Answer these questions.

   a. Who is the shortest player?   _____

   b. Who is the tallest player?   _____

   c. Which players are taller than number 23? _____

   d. Which player is the same height as number 11?__

   e. Which player is the same height as number 2?___

   f. How much taller is number 5 than number 10?____ in.

   g. How much taller is number 1 than number 10?____ in.

   h. Put the players in order from shortest to tallest.

      _____, _____, _____, _____, _____, _____, _____,

      _____, _____, _____, _____, _____

   i. Number 4 on the opposing team is 81 in. tall. How much taller is he than the Mighty Tigers' tallest player? _____ in.

2. Put the correct numbers on the jerseys of the tallest and shortest player on the team:

16

Name	**Date**

1. Televisions are measured by the diagonal width of their screens.

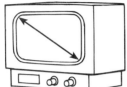

   a. Put these televisions in order of size from smallest to biggest screen, using the numbers 1 to 8.

TV SALE

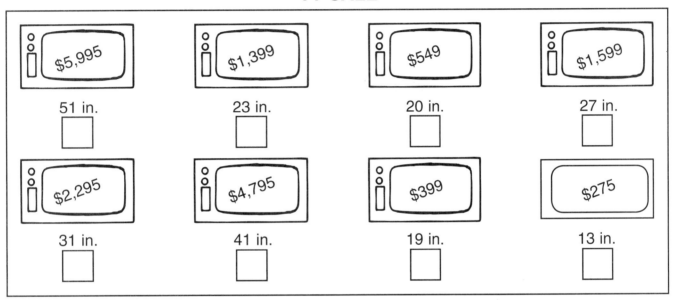

$5,995 $1,399 $549 $1,599

51 in.   23 in.   20 in.   27 in.

$2,295 $4,795 $399 $275

31 in.   41 in.   19 in.   13 in.

2. a. How much wider is the 27 in. than the 20 in. screen?

   number sentence: _____ ☐ in.

   b. How much wider is the 19 in. than the 13 in. screen?

   number sentence: _____ ☐ in.

   c. How much wider is the 31 in. than the 27 in. screen?

   number sentence: _____ ☐ in.

   d. How much wider is the 20 in. than the 13 in. screen?

   number sentence: _____ ☐ in.

   e. How much wider is the 51 in. than the 41 in. screen?

   number sentence: _____ ☐ in.

3. On a sheet of paper draw a television with an 8 in. screen and draw your favorite television program.

Name	**Date**

1. Draw these lengths using a ruler.

   a. 1 in.   •   •   •   •   •   •

   b. 2 in.   •   •   •   •   •   •

   c. ½ in.   •   •   •   •   •   •

   d. 2 ½ in.   •   •   •   •   •   •

   e. 3 in.   •   •   •   •   •   •

   f. 4 in.   •   •   •   •   •   •

   g. 5 in.   •   •   •   •   •   •

   h. 5 ½ in.   •   •   •   •   •   •

2. The perimeters of the following rectangles are given, together with the length of one side. Find the length of the longer side of each rectangle.

   a. Perimeter = 30 in.
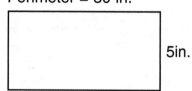
   5in.
   Length = _____

   b. Perimeter − 16 in.
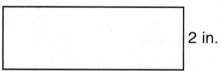
   2 in.
   Length = _____

   c. P = 50 in.
   7 in.
   Length = _____

   d. P = 40 in.

   9 in.
   Length = _____

18

Name	**Date**

> **12 inches (in.) = 1 foot (ft.)**
> **3 feet (ft.) = 1 yard (yd.)**

1. Solve these problems.   Work Space

   a. Julian cut 2 yards off a 10-yard plank. How long is the plank now?

   _____ yd.

   b. Alice swam 3 laps of the 9-yard pool. How many yards did she swim?

   _____ yd.

   c. Adam is 91 in. tall and Ben is 67 in. tall. How much taller is Adam?

   _____ ft.

   d. The height of a brick fence is going to be 124 in. The brick layers have built the wall to a height of 100 in. How many more to go?

   _____ ft.

   e. When Adrian planted a bush it was 20 in. high. It is now 56 in. high. How much has the bush grown?

   _____ ft.

   f. The garden is rectangular in shape. The longest side is 4 yards and the shortest is 3 yards. What is the perimeter of the garden?

   _____ yd.

   g. If Lily needs 3 yards of fabric for one dress, how many yards of fabric would she need for 4 dresses?

   _____ yd.

2. Make up a problem and get a friend to solve it.

19

Name   **Date**

1. Curtains come in different lengths called "drops". Draw lines from the windows to the drop that suits it best.

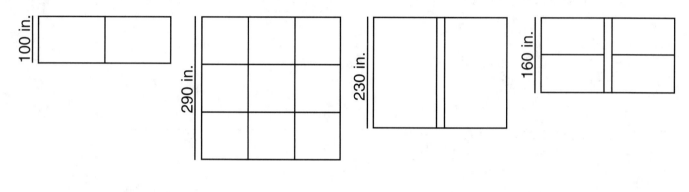

| 240 in. | 180 in. | 120 in. | 300 in. |

2. If each curtain shrank by 3 in., find the new lengths.

   a. 300 in.   **b.** 240 in.   **c.** 180 in.   **d.** 120 in.

   _____ in.   _____ in.   _____ in.   _____ in.

3. Use a calculator to find the perimeter of each mat. Estimate first.

   a. 235 in.   **b.** 230 in.   **c.** 230 in.

   165 in. [ ]   170 in. 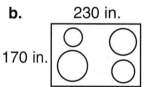   168 in. [hexagon]

   E _____ P _____   E _____ P _____   E _____ P _____

   d. 170 in.   **e.** 150 in.   **f.** 170 in.

   120 in. [ ]   132 in. 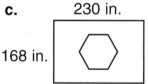   117 in. [hexagon]

   E _____ P _____   E _____ P _____   E _____ P _____

Name	**Date**

1. Write true or false.

    a. 1 yard is longer than 113 in. _____   **b.** 246 in. is taller than 199 in. _____

2.   **a.** 56 in. – 7 in. = _____   **b.** 105 in. + 82 in. = _____

3. Draw a line 4 in. long.

4. Find the perimeter of each shape.

   a.   **b.**   4 in.   **c.**   3.4 in.

3 in.   5 in.

     3 in.   7 in.   8.1 in.

    P = _____   P = _____

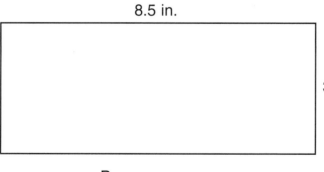

   d.   8.5 in.

                                     3.5 in.

                                                        P = _____

           P = _____

5.   **a.** 1/3 yd. = _____ in.   **b.** ½ ft. = _____ in.   **c.** ¾ ft. = _____ in.

6.   **a.** A square has a perimeter of 16 in. If one side is 4 in. long, how long are the other three sides? _____

    b. Yu Feng's fishing line was 50 yards long. It becomes tangled, so 7 yards have to be cut off the line. How long is the line now? _____

    c. Erin swam 100 yards, stopped for a rest, swam 50 yards and then another 100 yards. How many yards did she swim altogether? _____

                                        #8992 Targeting Math: Measurement

Name	**Date**

Equipment: 1 die, 1 small counter for each player.

Number of players: 2-4

Aim: To be the first to finish.

To start: Each player rolls the die. The highest scorer starts. Other players follow in a clockwise direction.

Reminders:
1 mile = 1,760 yards
1 yard = 3 feet
1 foot = 12 inches

Rules:
- Roll the die
- Move the number of spaces on the board.
- If you land on a measurement you must convert it: miles to yards, yards to feet; feet to inches.
- If you are correct, move forward one space. If you are wrong, move back one space. The other players are the judges.

73	74 19 ft.	75	76	77	78 20 mi.	79	80 100 yd.	81 FINISH
72 806 ft.	71	70 $\frac{3}{4}$ mi	69	68 $10\frac{1}{2}$ ft.	67	66	65 1 mi.	64
55	56	57 100 yd.	58	59	60 10 mi.	61	62	63 $\frac{1}{4}$ mi
54 14 ft.	53	52	51	50 8 mi.	49	48	47 18 yd.	46
37	38 $1\frac{2}{3}$ yd.	39	40	41 20 ft.	42	43	44	45 2 mi.
36	35	34 7 yd.	33	32	31	30 10 ft.	29	28
19 24 yd.	20	21	22	23 $\frac{1}{2}$ ft.	24	25	26 5 mi.	27
18	17	16	15 38 ft.	14	13	12 16 yd.	11	10
1 START	2 $2\frac{1}{2}$ yd.	3	4 30 ft.	5	6	7	8 5 ft.	9

INCHES, FEET, YARDS, AND MILES

Unit 3

Convert measurements
Perimeters
Interpreting
Estimating
Measuring in inches

Objectives

- makes conversions between measurement units.
- measures perimeter
- counts, compares and calculates with decimals (up to two places to the right of zero)
- selects and carries out the operation appropriate to situations involving addition and subtraction
- checks, using an alternative method if necessary, whether answers to problems are correct and sensible
- estimates, measures and records the length of objects in meters and centimeters
- uses number skills involving whole numbers to solve problems
- estimates, measures and records length in units from inches to miles
- represents, interprets and explains mathematical technology, including simple graphs and diagrams

Language

yards, inch, perimeter, tallest, shortest, longest, order, wing span, leg span, long, diameter, high, lowest, miles, how many?, difference

Materials/Resources

calculator, colored pencils, large sheets of paper

Contents of Student Pages

* Materials needed for each reproducible student page

Page 25 Inches and Feet
Convert inches to feet – feet to inches; find perimeters.

* calculators

Page 26 Problem Solving
Reading tables and answering questions; order lengths by interpreting information.

Page 27 Perimeters
Perimeters of sports fields – estimating then checking using a calculator.

* calculators

Page 28 Measuring Spans
Drawing given lengths.

* colored pencils, large sheets of paper

Page 29 Earth Facts
Using given information – about Earth's natural features; ordering lengths; using a calculator; solving subtraction problems.

* calculators

Page 30 Distance
Reading a map – miles; working out distances.

Page 31 Assessment

Remember

- ❑ Continue giving students opportunities to estimate lengths and then check their estimates.
- ❑ Ensure that students are aware of correct language in reading yards, e.g. 1.15 yd. is read as "one point one five yards."

Additional Activities

❏ Read the students part of *Gulliver's Travels* by Jonathan Swift and integrate with visual arts. Using student suggestions, illustrate the story.

❏ Divide students into groups and have each group research records, e.g. world, Olympic, for events such as high jump, long jump, pole vault, triple jump, javelin, shot put, hammer throw. Discuss. Report to class.

❏ Have a "mini" Olympics – plan events with students. e.g. javelin could be throwing a feather. Do as much measuring as possible.

❏ Look up records for length in the Guinness Book of Records. Provide opportunities for students to estimate and measure the lengths.

❏ Find reports in newspapers that mention distances, e.g. "the football player had a 50 yard throw." Read them to the students.

❏ Give students an opportunity to rule lines of different lengths to create a pattern.

❏ Students work in pairs. One names a length, the other draws the length. The first student checks the length. Then they swap.

❏ Divide students into groups and allow them to research animal migration. Discuss findings and lot migrations on a map.

❏ In Health/P.E. get students to estimate 100 yd., 200 yd., 400 yd., then check with a trundle wheel or measuring tape. Students can then walk/run the distance.

Answers

Page 25 Inches and Feet
1. a. 2 ft.
   b. ½ ft. or .5 ft.
   c. 3 ft.
   d. 5 ft.
   e. 13 ft.
   f. 8.5 ft. or 8 ½ ft.
   g. 4 ft.
   h. 17 ft.
2. a. 2 ft. 1 in.
   b. 1 in. 2 in.
   c. 8 ft. 9 in.
   d. 6 ft. 1 in.
   e. 4 ft. 0 in.
   f. 6 ft. 0 in.
   g. 16 ft. 2 in.
   h. 8 ft. 4 in.
3. a. 15.76 ft.
   b. 13.40 ft.
   c. 21.26 ft.
   d. 11.85 ft.
   e. 13.40 ft.

   f. 10.40 ft.
   g. c
   h. d

Page 26 Problem Solving
1. a. female blue whale
   b. starfish
   c. white shark, sperm whale, female blue whale
2. a. giraffe
   b. gorilla
   c. giraffe, elephant, Robert Wadlow, gorilla
3. a. Mike 8.96 yd.
   b. Mark 8.94 yd.
   c. Jesse 8.93 yd.

Page 27 Perimeters
1. a. 69.48 yd.
   b. 64.00 yd.
   c. 5.48 yd.
2. a. 91.4 yd.
   b. 358 yd.
   c. 292.6 yd.
   d. 420 yd.

Page 28 Measuring Spans
Teacher to check.

Page 29 Earth Facts
1. 2, 3, 1, 5, 4
2. 2,3,1
3. 1,3,2,5,4
4. a. 727 yd.
   b. 4,056 yd.
   c. 263 yd.

Page 30 Distance
1. a. lighthouse, 11 mi.
   b. 11 mi.
   c. 16 mi.
   d. 17 mi.

Page 31 Assessment
1. a. 3 ft.
   b. 2 ft.
   c. 4 ft.
   d. 6 ft.
   e. 9 ft.
   f. 1 ft.
2. a. 2 ft. 3 in.
   b. 3 ft. 4 in.
   c. 7 ft. 1 in.
   d. 8 ft. 4 in.
3. a. 17.2 in.
   b. 20 in.
   c. 13 in.
   d. 9.4 in.
4. a. 6 in.
   b. 21 in.
5. a. 6 ft.
   b. $1.00

#8992 Targeting Math: Measurement

Name	**Date**

12 inches (in.) = 1 foot (ft.)

1. Rewrite as feet.

   a. 24 inches _____ ft.   **b.** 6 inches _____ ft.

   c. 36 inches _____ ft.   **d.** 3 feet 24 inches _____ ft.

   e. 12 feet 12 inches _____ ft.   **f.** 8 feet 6 inches _____ ft.

   g. 48 inches _____ ft.   **h.** 14 feet 36 inches _____ ft.

2. Rewrite as feet and inches.

   a. 25 in. _____ ft. _____ in.   **b.** 14 in. _____ ft. _____ in.

   c. 7 ft. 21 in. _____ ft. _____ in.   **d.** 5 ft. 13 in. _____ ft. _____ in.

   e. 48 in. _____ ft. _____ in.   **f.** 72 in. _____ ft. _____ in.

   g. 14 ft. 26 in. _____ ft. _____ in.   **h.** 100 in. _____ ft. _____ in.

3. Find these perimeters. Use a calculator.

   a.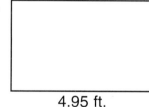
   2.93 ft.
   4.95 ft.

   Perimeter _____ ft.

   b.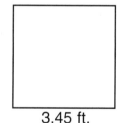
   3.25 ft.
   3.45 ft.

   Perimeter _____ ft.

   c.
   3.88 ft.
   6.75 ft.

   Perimeter _____ ft.

   d.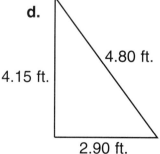
   4.80 ft.
   4.15 ft.
   2.90 ft.

   Perimeter _____ ft.

   e.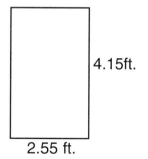
   4.15ft.
   2.55 ft.

   Perimeter _____ ft.

   f.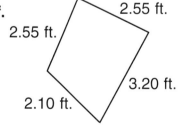
   2.55 ft.
   2.55 ft.
   3.20 ft.
   2.10 ft.

   Perimeter _____ ft.

   g. Which shape has the biggest perimeter? [ ]

   h. Which shape has the smallest perimeter? [ ]

(25)

Name	**Date**

1. Look at this table showing the lengths of different animals. Answer the questions.

Female blue whale	33.58 yd.
Polar bear	3.4 yd.
Sperm whale	20.7 yd.
Siberian tiger	3.15 yd.
White shark	12.65 yd.
Snake	10 yd.
Starfish	1.38 yd.

  a. Which is the longest?_____

  b. Which is the shortest? _____

  c. Which animals are longer than the snake?

    _____

    _____

2. Look at this table showing heights and answer these questions.

Elephant 3.7 yd.	Giraffe 5.3 yd.
Gorilla 1.95 yd.	Robert Wadlow 2.7 yd.

  a. Which is the tallest?_____

  b. Which is the shortest? _____

  c. Order from tallest to shortest. _____

3. In a long jump event, each entrant has three jumps. Each entrant is placed according to his best jump. Look at these results and decide who wins 1st, 2nd and 3rd places.

Jesse	Peter	Mike	Trent	Mark
8.93 yd.	8.90 yd.	8.91 yd.	8.90 yd.	8.92 yd.
8.91 yd.	8.89 yd.	8.90 yd.	7.79 yd.	8.94 yd.
8.90 yd.	8.90 yd.	8.96 yd.	8.69 yd.	8.91 yd.

* World Record *

  a. 1st place _____ with a jump of _____ yd.

  b. 2nd place _____ with a jump of _____ yd.

  c. 3rd place _____ with a jump of _____ yd.

26

Name	**Date**

1. Estimate and then find the perimeters. Use a calculator to check.

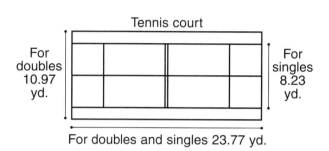

Tennis court

For doubles 10.97 yd.

For singles 8.23 yd.

For doubles and singles 23.77 yd.

a. Find the perimeter of the doubles court.

Estimate   Actual

yd.   yd.

b. Find the perimeter of the singles court.

Estimate   Actual

yd.   yd.

c. How much bigger is the doubles court?

Estimate   Actual

yd.   yd.

2.   **a.** Basketball court   **b.** Football field   **c.** Hockey field   **d.** Soccer field

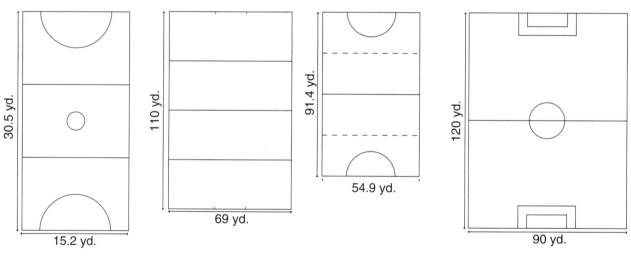

30.5 yd.   15.2 yd.

110 yd.   69 yd.

91.4 yd.   54.9 yd.

120 yd.   90 yd.

a. Estimate _____

Actual yd. _____

b. Estimate _____

Actual yd. _____

c. Estimate _____

Actual yd. _____

d. Estimate _____

Actual yd. _____

27

Name	**Date**

You need to measure across the widest part.

You need a pencil, colored pencils, large sheets of paper.

1. Using the information, measure and draw these creatures.

   a. The world's largest known spider is the goliath bird-eating spider. It has a leg span of 11 in.

   b. The largest fly has a wingspan of about 4 in.

   c. The Queen Alexandra bird wing butterfly can have a wingspan of 11 in.

   d. The bee hummingbird (a bird) has a wingspan of about 2.2 in.

   e. A Yorkshire terrier (dog) was 2.5 in. tall and 3.7 in. long.

   f. The smallest cat is 3 in. tall and 7.5 in. long.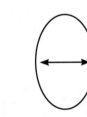

   g. The smallest horse (called "Little Pumpkin") stood 14 in. high.

2. Draw these eggs using the information.

   a. A dinosaur egg was about 8 in. long.   length   diameter

   b. The vervain hummingbird's egg is .5 in. long.

   c. An ostrich egg can be 8 in. long and have a diameter of 6 in.

Name   **Date**

1. Here is a list of some of the longest rivers in the world. Order from shortest to longest using the numbers 1 – 5.

   Mackenzie (Canada)   2,635 mi. ☐

   Yangtze (China)   3,430 mi. ☐

   Mekong (Asia)   2,600 mi. ☐

   Nile (Africa)   4,157 mi. ☐

   Mississippi-Missouri (USA) 4,082 mi. ☐

2. Here is a list of major waterfalls. Order from lowest to highest using the numbers 1 – 3.

   Tugela Falls (Africa)   1,037 yd. ☐

   Angel Falls (Venezuela)   1,071 yd. ☐

   Yosemite Falls (USA)   808 yd. ☐

3. Here is a list of some of the highest mountains in the world. Order from shortest to highest using the numbers 1 – 5.

   Vinson Massif (Antarctica)   5,620 yd. ☐

   McKinley (USA)   6,774 yd. ☐

   Kilimanjaro (Africa)   6,447 yd. ☐

   Everest (Nepal/Tibet)   9,676 yd. ☐

   Aconcagua (Argentina)   7,611 yd. ☐

4. Use the back of this page to solve these problems.

   a. If the Nile is 4,157 mi. long and the Yangtze is 3,430 mi. long, use a calculator to find the difference in their lengths.

   ☐ mi.

   b. If Everest is 9,676 yd. high and Vinson Massif is 5,620 yd. high, use a calculator to find the difference in their heights.

   ☐ yd.

   c. Using a calculator, find the difference in height between Yosemite Falls and Angel Falls.

   ☐ yd.

   d. Choose one of these rivers, waterfalls, or mountains and find out more about it. (29)

Name   **Date**

1. Susan and Kate rode their bikes while on holidays on Adventure Island.

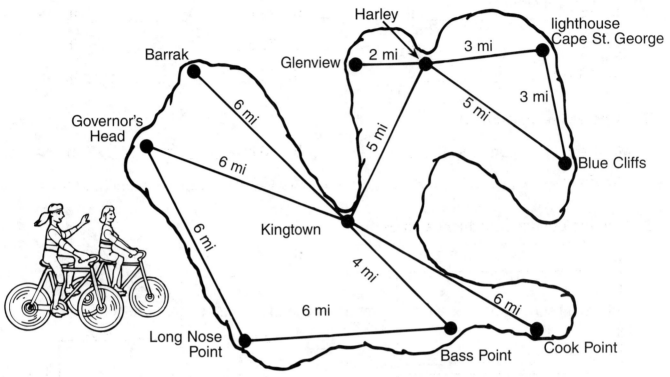

   a. On Monday they rode from Harley to Cape St. George, looked at the _____,
   rode 3 mi. to Blue Cliffs and had lunch. After lunch they took the shortest way back
   to Harley. How many mi. did they ride?

   ☐ mi.

   b. On Tuesday they rode from Harley to Kingtown and then to Governor's Head. They
   decided to stop there overnight. How many mi. did they ride?

   ☐ mi.

   c. On Wednesday they rode from Governor's Head to Long Nose Point and then to
   Bass Point. They then rode the shortest way back to Kingtown. How many mi. did
   they ride?

   ☐ mi.

   d. On Thursday they rode from Kingtown to Cook Point and had lunch. After lunch they
   rode back to Kingtown and then back to Harley. How many mi. did they ride?

   ☐ mi.

30

Name	**Date**

1. Write the following lengths in feet.

   a. 36 in. _____ ft.   **b.** 24 in. _____ ft.

   c. 48 in. _____ ft.   **d.** 72 in. _____ ft.

   e. 108 in. _____ ft.   **f.** 12 in. _____ ft.

2. Write as inches and feet.

   a. 27 in. _____ ft. _____ in.   **b.** 40 in. _____ ft. _____ in.

   c. 85 in. _____ ft. _____ in.   **d.** 100 in. _____ ft. _____ in.

3. Find the perimeter of these shapes

   a.   6 in.

2.6 in.

   b.   2 in.

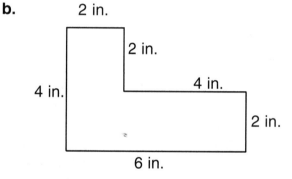

2 in.

4 in.   4 in.

2 in.

6 in.

   P = _____   P = _____

   c.   5 in.

1.5 in.

   d.   3.3 in.

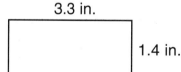

1.4 in.

   P = _____   P = _____

4. **a.** ½ ft. = _____ in.   **b.** 1 ¾ ft. = _____ in.

5. **a.** Brendon had a length of string 8 ft. long. He cut off ¼ of the length. How long is the length of string now? _____

   b. A yard of fabric costs $2. What is the cost of half a yard? _____

31

AREA

These black line masters provide opportunities to estimate, measure, order and compare areas using formal and informal units of measurement.

Students are involved in decision-making and lateral-thinking activities based on boundaries and tessellations.

Square feet and square inches are investigated and used in problem solving activities.

There are two assessment pages and an activity, which involves manipulating shapes to fill a given area.

INFORMAL UNITS OF AREA

Unit 1

Tessellation
Comparing
Boundaries
Informal units
Ordering

Objectives

- demonstrates an understanding of the concepts of area, boundaries and tessellations
- can relate the concept of area to everyday situations
- can measure, and compare areas of shapes using informal areas
- can show a relationship between the boundary of a shape and its area

Language

unit of measure, area, surface, tessellation, measuring tool, unit cubes, boundary, overlapping

Materials/Resources

colored pencils, leaves, Base 10 materials (centicubes/ unit cubes), ruler, scissors

Contents of Student Pages

* Materials needed for each reproducible student page

. . . .
Remember

❑ Measurement is a hands-on experience.
❑ Allow children plenty of time to make their own discoveries.

Additional Activities

❏ Write a list of jobs or professions that use area in their workplaces.

❏ Compare the areas of the different continents of the world. Order these from smallest to largest.

❏ Make a wall hanging of every child's hand print. Reduce the gaps between each hand print as much as possible. Calculate the total area.

❏ Each child draws the tiles that are on his/her bathroom or kitchen walls or floor. Discuss why these are tessellations.

❏ Looking for tessellating patterns in magazines, etc. Make a class poster.

Answers

Page 35 Looking at Area
1. Teacher to check.
2. Teacher to check.
3. a. painter
   b. farmer
   c. tiler/plumber
   d. builder/quantity surveyor
   e. carpet layer

Page 36 Informal Units
Teacher to check.

Page 37 Boundaries
Teacher to check.

Page 38 Thinking About Area
1. Teacher to check.
2. a. from left to right: 3, 2, 4, 5, 1
   b. from left to right: 3, 4, 1, 5, 2
   c. from left to right: 2, 1, 4, 5, 3
3. Teacher to check.

Page 39 Tessellations
1. a-d. Teacher to check.
2. check b, c, d, f
3. a. slide
   b. slide
   c. flip and slide
   d. turn
4. Teacher to check.
5. Teacher to check.

Page 40 Assessment
1. a. from left to right 3, 2, 5, 4, 1
   b. from left to right 2, 1, 4, 3
   c. from left to right 2, 3, 4, 1, 5
2. a. 33 ft.^{2}
   b. 215 in.^{2}
   c. 4 ¾ ft.^{2}
   d. 10.6 in.^{2}
   e. 1600 ft.^{2}
3. a, c, d
4. Teacher to check.
5. Teacher to check.
6. Teacher to check.
7. Teacher to check.

Page 41 Activity Page—Creating a Rectangle
Teacher to check.

34

Name	**Date**

1. Circle the shape inside each box that has the greatest area.

 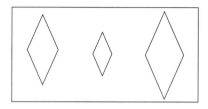 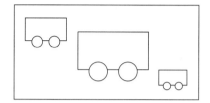

2. Surface is another word for area. Color the object with the greatest surface red and the smallest blue.

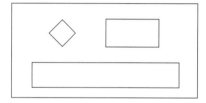 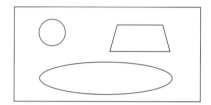 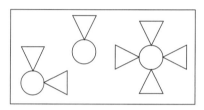

3. For many people it is important to understand area and how to work it out. Read the following statements and see if you can work out who these people are.

   a. I use area to work out how many cans of paint I will need to paint all the walls in Mrs. Nesbitt's house. I am a _____.

   b. I need to understand the area of my land so I can calculate the amount of seeds and fertilizer I will need to buy. I am a _____.

   c. I want to tile Mr. Gregory's bathroom, so I must calculate the area of the walls and floor. Then I can work out how many tiles I will need for the job. I am a _____.

   d. The cement mixer is arriving next week to pour concrete on the floor of the house I am building. I need to understand area to work out how much cement I should order. I am a _____.

   e. Mrs. Browning has chosen a lovely dark green carpet to replace the cream-colored mats in her apartment. I have to measure each room to work out the total area of carpet needed to make her apartment look smart. I am a _____.

35

Name	**Date**

Collect 10 leaves from one of the trees in your school playground.

1. Cover the following objects with the leaves and record how many were needed.

   Number of Leaves

   a. your desk top   _____

   b. your pencil case   _____

   c. your math book   _____

   d. Did everyone in the class choose leaves of the same size and shape? _____

   e. Did everyone in the class get the same answers? _____

   f. Why? _____

   _____

2. Use your hands to cover the same objects. Record your answers.

   Number of Hands

   a. your desk top   _____

   b. your pencil case   _____

   c. your math book   _____

   d. Were these results more alike? _____

3. Now use "hundreds" blocks to cover the same 3 objects.

   Number of Hundreds

   a. your desk top   _____

   b. your pencil case   _____

   c. your math book   _____

   d. Which was the best and easiest measuring tool? Circle your choice.

         leaves   hands   hundreds

   e. Why? _____

   _____

| **Name** | **Date** |

1. Use a colored pencil to draw a dotted line around the outside boundary of these shapes.

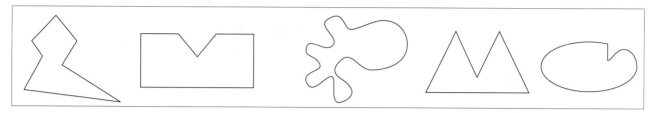

2. Join the dots below in any way you like to make 2 different shapes. In the first box the sheep should be inside the boundary of one of your shapes. In the second box place the sheep outside the boundary of your shapes.

   a.   b.

3. Join some dots so that the sheep is inside the boundary of 2 different shapes. i.e. The two shapes should overlap.

   Go back and look at all the shapes you have created. Color the one with the smallest area.

4. Write three examples of boundaries. (Example: boundaries in a dodge ball game.)

   a. _____

   b. _____

   c. _____

37

Name	**Date**

1. Finish the boundaries of these shapes so the areas increase in each frame.

    a.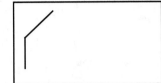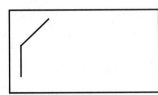

    b.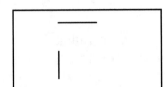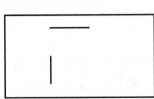

2. Order these shapes from the smallest to the largest area. Use the numbers 1-5.

    a.

    b.

    c.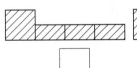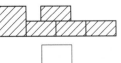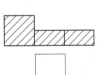

3. Draw a shape on the left that has a smaller area and one on the right that has a greater area.

    a.   **b.**

    c.   **d.**

Name	**Date**

1. Continue these shapes to create tessellating patterns.

   a. 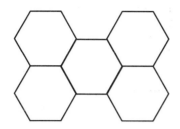   **b.**

   c. 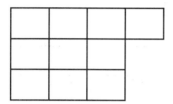   **d.**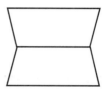

2. Place a check √ under each shape that will tessellate.

   a.   **b.**   **c.**   **d.**   **e.**   **f.**

3. Tessellations can be made by sliding, flipping or turning a shape. Look at these letters. State whether they have been flipped, slid, or turned.

   a. 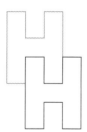   **b.**    **c.** 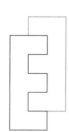   **d.**

   _____   _____   _____   _____

4. List 5 capital letters that will not tessellate.

   _____ _____ _____ _____ _____

5. Name 2 places in your home where tessellating patterns are used.

   _____   _____

#8992 Targeting Math: Measurement

Name	**Date**

1. Order these shapes from smallest to largest area.

   a.

   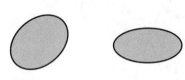  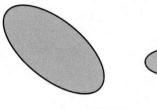

   ___ ___ ___ ___ ___

   b.

   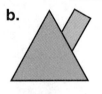 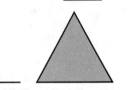  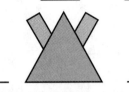

   ___ ___ ___ ___ ___

   c.

   ___ ___ ___ ___ ___

2. Rewrite in the short form:

   a. thirty-three square feet _____

   b. two hundred and fifteen square inches _____

   c. four and three-quarter square feet _____

   d. ten point six square inches _____

   e. one thousand six hundred square feet _____

3. Circle the letters of the tessellating patterns

   a. 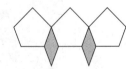   **b.** 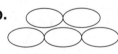   **c.**   **d.**

4. Name 4 objects that could be used as informal measuring units, (example: leaves).

   _____ _____ _____ _____

5. Name 2 objects that would be good measuring tools.

   _____ _____

6. **a.** What is a boundary? _____

   _____

   b. Give 2 examples. _____

7. Draw your own tessellating pattern on the back of this page.

40

Name	**Date**

1. Draw a rectangle 12 cm (centimeters) long and 8 cm wide.

2. Cut out these pieces. Put them together to fill your rectangle. Remember – no gaps and no overlaps!

41

FORMAL UNITS OF AREA

Unit 2

**Formal units
Calculating area
Irregular shapes
Square foot
Square inch
Problems**

Objectives

- explains the need for a formal unit of measure
- calculates area with formal units
- demonstrates an understanding of a square foot and a square inch
- records area using numerals and short method, (example ft.^{2} , in.^{2})
- applies knowledge of square inches to creating shapes

Language

calculate, formal, informal units, square foot, square inch, increase, decrease, grid paper, half, greater than, smaller than, approximately

Materials/Resources

scissors, large sheets of paper, sticky tape, ruler

Contents of Student Pages

* Materials needed for each reproducible student page

Page 44 Calculating Area
An introduction to formal units; counting squares covered by shapes.

Page 45 Area of Irregular Shapes
Counting squares and half squares.

Page 46 The Square Foot
Creating a square foot; calculating and estimating.

* sticky tape and scissors, large sheets of paper, ruler

Page 47 The Square Inch
Drawing square inches; choosing the best unit of measure.

Page 48 Area Problems
A variety of written problems that require a basic knowledge of area.

Page 49 Assessment

Remember

- ❑ All lines should be ruled with a sharp pencil.
- ❑ Reinforce difference between area and perimeter.

Additional Activities

❑ *Research the areas of other countries. The Internet could be used. What other units of measure area used for large areas?*

❑ *Place a square foot of paper on the ground and see how many students can be squeezed onto this space.*

❑ *Ask a member of the local council to visit to explain council boundaries and the population per square foot/mile.*

❑ *Research when it first became important to measure area and why. What were early measuring tools and measurements?*

Answers

Page 44 Calculating Area
1. 9
2. 22
3. 23
4. 42
5. 30

Page 45 Area of Irregular Shapes
1. 7
2. 19
3. 18
4. 21
5. 18
6. 12
7. 29 1/2

Page 46 The Square Foot
1. Teacher to check.
2. Teacher to check.
3. Teacher to check.
4. a. 307 ft.^{2}
   b. 26 ½ ft.^{2}
   c. 88 ft.^{2}
   d. 511 ft.^{2}
   e. 1.6 ft.^{2}
5. yes

Page 47 The Square Inch
1. Teacher to check.
2. a. 22 in.^{2}
   b. 19 ft.^{2}
   c. 9 ft.^{2}
   d. 17 in.^{2}
   e. 13 ½ in.^{2}
   f. 85 in.^{2}
3. a. ft.^{2}
   b. ft.^{2}
   c. ft.^{2}
   d. in.^{2}
   e. in.^{2}
   f. in.^{2}
   g. in.^{2}
   h. in.^{2}
   i. ft.^{2}

Page 48 Area Problems
1. a. 100 ft.^{2}
   b. Teacher to check.
   c. 10,400 ft.^{2}
   d. 180 ft.^{2}
   e. 1,000 ft.^{2}
   f. 29 ft.^{2}

Page 49 Assessment
1. a. <
   b. >
   c. <
   d. >
   e. >
   f. >
2. a. 13 squares
   b. 21 squares
   c. 10 squares
3. Teacher to check.
4. a. ft.^{2}
   b. ft.^{2}
   c. in.^{2}
   d. in.^{2}
   e. ft.^{2}
   f. in.^{2}

43

Name   **Date**

Calculate the areas of the shapes below by counting the number of squares.

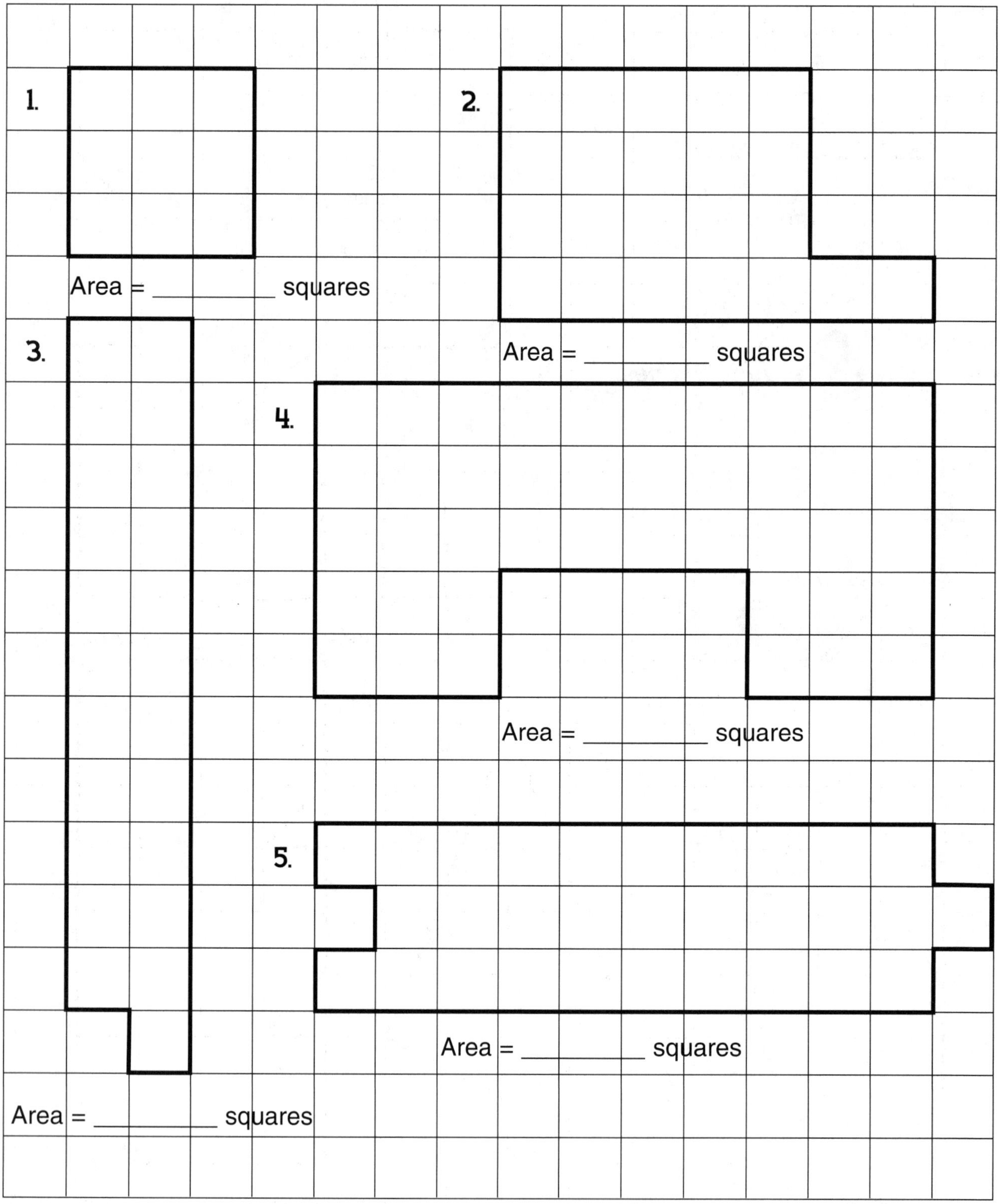

1.

Area = _____ squares

2.

Area = _____ squares

3.

4.

Area = _____ squares

5.

Area = _____ squares

Area = _____ squares

Name	**Date**

Carefully calculate the number of squares that each of these shapes cover. Don't forget to add the half squares.

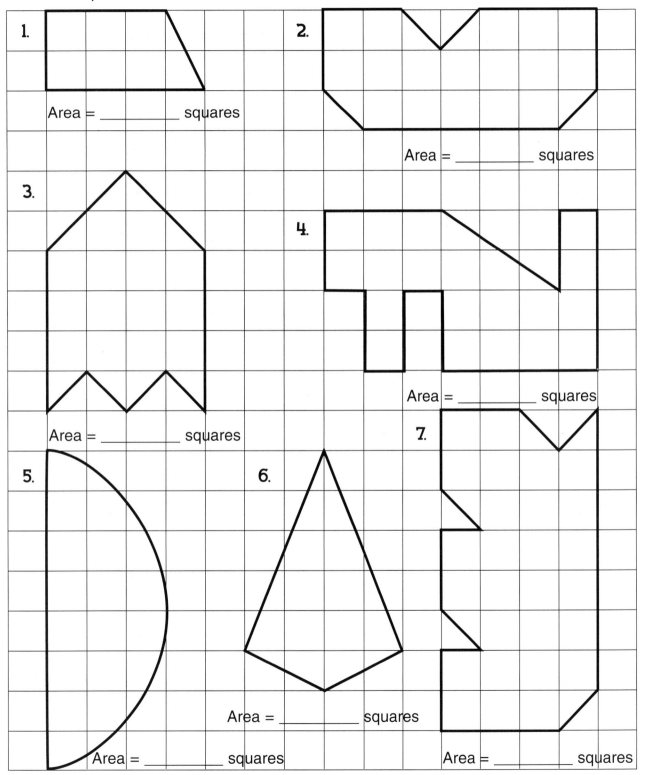

1.

Area = _____ squares

2.

Area = _____ squares

3.

Area = _____ squares

4.

Area = _____ squares

7.

5.

6.

Area = _____ squares

Area = _____ squares

Area = _____ squares

Area = _____ squares

45

Name	**Date**

1. Using a ruler and large sheets of paper, create a square foot. Use this to estimate the following.

   How many square feet would cover:

   a. your classroom floor?   _____

   b. your gym floor?   _____

   c. the board?   _____

   d. the classroom door?   _____

2. List 5 things in your classroom that have an area of less than 1 square foot.

   a. _____ **b.** _____ **c.** _____

   d. _____ **e.** _____

3. Fold your square foot into quarters. Find 5 things outside your classroom that have an area of less than a quarter of a square foot.

   a. _____ **b.** _____ **c.** _____

   d. _____ **e.** _____

4. Rewrite these the short way. Example: seventeen square feet = 17 ft.^2

   a. three hundred and seven square feet   =   _____

   b. twenty-six and a half square feet   =   _____

   c. eighty-eight square feet   =   _____

   d. five hundred and eleven square feet   =   _____

   e. one point six square feet   =   _____

5. Cut your square foot into 6 pieces. Using sticky tape, stick it back together in a different way. Is it still a square foot? _____

(46)

Name	**Date**

A square inch is much smaller than a square foot.

A square inch is used to measure the area of smaller objects.

1. Use a ruler to draw one square inch.

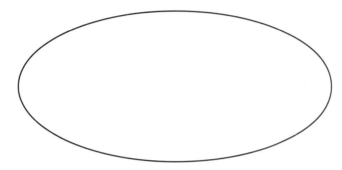

2. Increase or decrease these areas by the amount shown. Watch the units being used.

   Example: 5 in.^{2} increase 2 in.^{2} = 7 in.^{2}

   a. 15 in.^{2} increase 7 in.^{2} = _____

   b. 25 ft.^{2} decrease 6 ft.^{2} = _____

   c. 6 ½ ft.^{2} increase 2 ½ ft.^{2} = _____

   d. 26 in.^{2} decrease 9 in.^{2} =_____

   e. 2 ½ in.^{2} increase 11 in.^{2} = _____

   f. 106 in.^{2} decrease 21 in.^{2} =_____

3. Choose the best unit of measure (in.^{2} or ft.^{2}) for the area of each of these:

   a. picnic blanket   _____

   b. football field   _____

   c. a farm   _____

   d. computer screen   _____

   e. DVD box   _____

   f. a page out of a novel   _____

   g. slice of bread   _____

   h. a man's mustache   _____

   i. a carpet in a house   _____

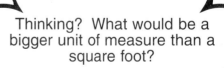

Thinking? What would be a bigger unit of measure than a square foot?

_____

What would be smaller than 1 in.^{2}?

_____

(47)

                          #8992 Targeting Math: Measurement

Name	**Date**

1. Use your knowledge of area to solve these. Show your work.

   a. My uncle has a backyard half the size of mine. If my backyard is 200 ft.^{2} how big is his?

   b. Susan has just drawn a closed shape with 5 boundaries. Draw what her shape might look like.

   c. Farmer Weston's farm is 8,100 ft.^{2}. He has bought the farm next door that is 2,300 ft.^{2}. How much land does he have now?

   d. One can of paint covers an area of 60 ft.^{2}. What area will be covered by three cans of paint?

   e. The school playground has an area of 3,000 ft.^{2}. This must be divided into 3 equal playing spaces. What area will each new playground cover?

   f. The area of my bathroom floor is 35 ½ ft.^{2}. The bath takes up 6 ½ ft.^{2} of this space. The rest of the floor will need to be tiled. What is the area of the rest of the floor?

#8992 Targeting Math: Measurement

Name	**Date**

1. Use greater than (>) or less than (<) to make these statements true.

   a. The area of a matchbox is _____ than the area of a blanket.

   b. The area of the school hall is _____ than the area of my bed.

   c. The area of the football field is _____ than the total area of the United States.

   d. The area of a quarter is _____ than the area of a dime.

   e. The area of this page is _____ than the area of a $100 bill.

   f. The area of a desk is _____ than the area of a video game box.

2. Calculate the areas of these shapes.

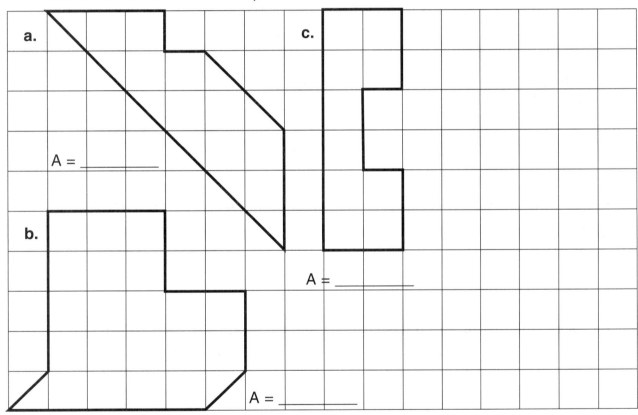

a. A = _____

b. A = _____

c. A = _____

3. On the grid paper above, draw:

   a. a shape with straight sides that covers 11 ½ units^2.

   b. a shape with curved sides that covers approximately 7 units^2.

4. Would you use ft.^{2} or in.^{2} for the area of:

   a. the local park? _____

   b. the bathroom floor? _____

   c. a ruler? _____

   d. a small towel? _____

   e. a slide? _____

   f. a book cover? _____

49

MASS

These units contain exercises to reinforce the concept that size does not always relate directly to mass.

Skills include measuring, estimating, approximating and comparing and ordering masses. Ounces and pounds are used, written in both long and short forms, and added and subtracted.

Problem solving uses masses in real life situations and also in graphing and money.

Two assessment pages and an activity are included.

#8992 Targeting Math: Measurement

MEASURING AND PROBLEM SOLVING WITH MASS

Unit 1

**Counting
Pounds
Money
Addition
Interpreting graphs
Problem solving
Calculators
Estimating**

Objectives

- approximates, counts, compares, orders and represents whole numbers and groups to 100
- estimates, compares and records the mass of objects to the nearest pound and recognizes the need for a unit smaller than the pound
- selects and carries out the operation appropriate to situations involving addition and subtraction
- uses understood written methods to add and subtract any whole numbers
- represents, interprets and explains mathematical situations using everyday language with some mathematical terminology, including simple graphs and diagrams
- uses number skills involving whole numbers to solve problems
- uses available technology to help in the solution of mathematical problems
- uses a calculator for operating on whole numbers, amounts of money and measurements

Language

mass, masses, balance, pounds, total mass, difference, greatest mass, least mass, take away, minus, how many?, left, estimate, actual, most expensive, cheapest, cost, round off

Materials/Resources

Base 10 materials (unit cubes/centicubes), colored pencils, calculators

Contents of Student Pages

- ★ Materials needed for each reproducible student page

Page 53 Masses in Pounds
Counting pound masses – coloring the correct numbers; adding pounds.
- ★ colored pencils

Page 54 Graphs
Making graphs – from information given; interpreting the graph.
- ★ Base 10 materials, colored pencils

Page 55 Problem Solving with Mass
Problems involving estimation and money.

Page 56 Assessment
- ★ calculator

Page 57 Activity Page—Books and Worms
Finding the masses of books and worms.

Remember

- ❏ Link with other math strands, e.g. number, including money.
- ❏ Be sensitive to student's feelings regarding their weight.
- ❏ Provide many types of experiences where comparison of mass is made so students realize that quantity is not linked to mass.
- ❏ Provide many experiences with informal units so students come to appreciate the need for a formal mass unit.

(51)

Additional Activities

- ❏ Give students many opportunities to estimate and then check the mass of different objects by using either informal or standard units.
- ❏ Encourage students to write their own mass problems and share them with the class.
- ❏ Provide students with food catalogues and encourage them to cut out and to group and pastes different masses, (example: 1 lb., 4 lbs.).
- ❏ If you do not have a student in your class with a weight problem, weigh everyone. Record the results in the form of a graph.
- ❏ Provide students with opportunities to lift different pound masses.
- ❏ Encourage students to look up the Guinness Book of Records to find interesting mass facts. These can be shared with the class.
- ❏ Brainstorm and complete a list with the students of items sold by the pound. Add to the list when new items are found.
- ❏ Encourage students to find out what their mass was as a baby. Record the results.
- ❏ Relate mass to everyday situations such as shopping. Make use of catalogues to compare prices and discuss "best buys".
- ❏ Provide opportunities for students to compare sizes of packaging for similar masses, (example: 1 lb., 2 lb. packs).

Answers

Page 53 Masses in Pounds
1. Teacher to check.
2. a. 48 lbs.
   b. 13 lbs.
   c. 62 lbs.

Page 54 Graphs
1. a. African lion
   b. St. Bernard dog
   c. Siberian Tiger
2. a. 45 lbs.
   b. 110 lbs.
   c. 380 lbs.
   d. 285 lbs.
3. Teacher to check.
4. Teacher to check.

Page 55 Problem Solving with Mass
1. a. 6 lbs.
   b. 14 lbs.
   c. 11 lbs.
   d. 14 lbs.
   e. 8 lbs.
   f. 9 lbs.
2. a. 30 lbs.
   b. 40 lbs.
   c. 30 lbs.
   d. 61 lbs.
3. a. $12
   b. $22
   c. $19

Page 56 Assessment
1. Teacher to check.
2. 24 lbs.
3. a. 7 lbs.
   b. 19 lbs.
   c. 2 lbs.
   d. 20 lbs.
   e. 5 lbs.
   f. 12 lbs.
4. a. 45 lbs.
   b. 42 lbs.
   c. 26 lbs.
   d. 84 lbs.
   e. 54 lbs.
   f. 53 lbs.
   g. 28 lbs.
   h. 35 lbs.
   i. 14 lbs.
   j. 60 lbs.
   k. 210 lbs.
   l. 166 lbs.
5. a. 231 lbs.
   b. 2,173 lbs.
   c. 693 lbs.
   d. 1,136 lbs.

Page 57 Activity Page—Books and Worms
1. 4 worms, 8 lbs., 4 lbs.
2. 7 worms, 6 lbs., 3 lbs.
3. 7 worms, 10 lbs., 5 lbs.
4. 3 worms, 4 lbs., 2 lbs.
5. 4 worms, 10 lbs., 5 lbs.

#8992 Targeting Math: Measurement

Name	**Date**

1. Color to show these masses.

   a. 98 lbs.

   b. 54 lbs.

   c. 21 lbs.

   d. 15 lbs.

2. Write the masses of the shaded weights.

   a.

   _____ lbs.

   b.

   _____ lbs.

   c.

   _____ lbs.

(53)

Name	**Date**

1. Here is a list of animals and their masses.

Gorilla	375 lbs.
Siberian Tiger	420 lbs.
Snake	485 lbs.
St. Bernard Dog	200 lbs.
African Lion	730 lbs.
Komodo Dragon	350 lbs.
Tortoise	485 lbs.

a. Which animal has the greatest mass?

_____

b. Which animal has the least mass?

_____

c. Which animal has a mass of 420 lbs.?

_____

2. Using Base 10 materials (centicubes/unit cubes) find the answers to these questions.

a. What is the difference in mass between the Siberian Tiger and the Gorilla?

_____ - _____ = _____ lbs.

b. What is the difference in mass between the Tortoise and the Gorilla?

_____ - _____ = _____ lbs.

c. What is the difference in mass between the African Lion and the Komodo Dragon?

_____ - _____ = _____ lbs.

d. What is the difference in mass between the Tortoise and the St. Bernard Dog?

_____ - _____ = _____ lbs.

3. Make a graph by coloring in the squares.

4. Write a question for your graph.

Mass of Animals

Pounds: 800, 780, 760, 740, 720, 700, 680, 660, 640, 620, 600, 580, 560, 540, 520, 500, 480, 460, 440, 420, 400, 380, 360, 340, 320, 300, 280, 260, 240, 220, 200

Animals: Gorilla, Tiger, Snake, Dog, Lion, Dragon, Tortoise

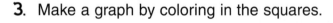

#8992 Targeting Math: Measurement

Name	Date

1. Solve these problems.

    a. 16 lbs. take away 10 lbs. _____

    b. take 5 lbs. from 19 lbs. _____

    c. 18 lbs. minus 7 lbs. _____

    d. 20 lbs. subtract 6 lbs. _____

    e. 24 lbs. take away 16 lbs. _____

    f. take 11 lbs. from 20 lbs. _____

2. **a.** There is a box with 46 lbs. of biscuits.

    16 lbs. are broken.

    How many are not broken? _____

    b. A bakery has 60 lbs. of flour.

    20 lbs. are used to make bread.

    How much flour is left? _____

    c. A restaurant has 53 lbs. of oranges.

    23 lbs. are juiced.

    How many lbs. of oranges are left?

    _____

    d. Paul has a mass of 76 lbs.

    and loses 15 lbs.

    What is Paul's new mass? _____

3.

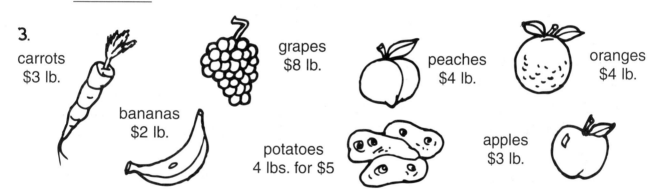

carrots $3 lb.   grapes $8 lb.   peaches $4 lb.   oranges $4 lb.

bananas $2 lb.   potatoes 4 lbs. for $5   apples $3 lb.

Estimate how much each person spent at the fruit and vegetable shop and then find the actual amount.

	Estimate	Actual
a. Cathy bought: 1 lb. of carrots, 2 lbs. of bananas, 4 lbs. of potatoes.		
b. Andres bought: 1 lb. of oranges, 1 lb. of peaches, 1 lb. of grapes, 2 lbs. of apples.		
c. Mitchell bought: 4 lbs. of potatoes, 1 lb. of peaches, 2 lbs. of apples, 2 lbs. of bananas.		

55

Name	**Date**

1. Color the weights that would balance this mass.

   89 lbs.

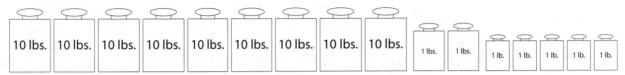

2. Write this mass.

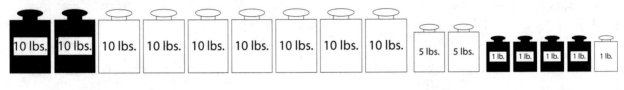

   _____ lbs.

3. Use the short form to write masses.

   a. 7 pounds   _____   b. 19 pounds   _____

   c. two pounds   _____   d. twenty pounds   _____

   e. 5 pounds   _____   f. twelve pounds   _____

4. Use a calculator to find the answers.

   a. 21 lbs. + 24 lbs. = _____ lbs.   b. 14 lbs. + 28 lbs. = _____ lbs.

   c. 10 lbs. + 16 lbs. = _____ lbs.   d. 70 lbs. + 14 lbs. = _____ lbs.

   e. 14 lbs. + 40 lbs. = _____ lbs.   f. 23 lbs. + 30 lbs. = _____ lbs.

   g. 84 lbs. – 56 lbs. = _____ lbs.   h. 68 lbs. – 33 lbs. = _____ lbs.

   i. 36 lbs. – 22 lbs. = _____ lbs.   j. 100 lbs. – 40 lbs. = _____ lbs.

   k. 490 lbs. – 280 lbs. = _____ lbs.   l. 726 lbs. – 560 lbs. = _____ lbs.

5. Solve these problems.

   a. One dog has a mass of 66 lbs., another 77 lbs. and another dog has a mass of 88 lbs. What is the total mass of the dogs? _____ lbs.

   b. The heaviest man was 974 lbs. and the heaviest woman was 1,199 lbs. What is their total mass? _____ lbs.

   c. The zoo has two gorillas. One has a mass of 353 lbs., the other a mass of 340 lbs. What is the total mass of the gorillas? _____ lbs.

   d. The zoo has three Siberian tigers – one is 397 lbs., one is 375 lbs., and another is 364 lbs. What is the total mass of the tigers? _____ lbs.

56

Name	**Date**

Books and worms have different masses. The mass of 1 book is always the same as 2 worms.

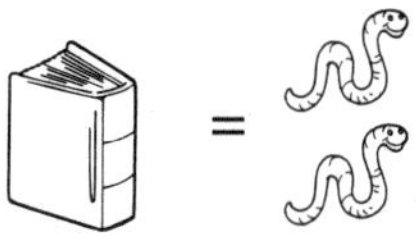

= 🪱🪱

Work out how many worms are needed to balance the scales for each question. Then write how much each book and worm weighs.

1. If [book]🪱🪱 = 16 lbs. 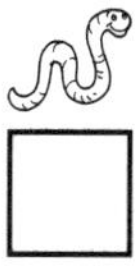   🪱 □ = 16 lbs.

   [book] = _____   🪱 = _____

2. If [book][book][book] 🪱 = 21 lbs. 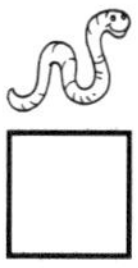   🪱 □ = 21 lbs.

   [book] = _____   🪱 = _____

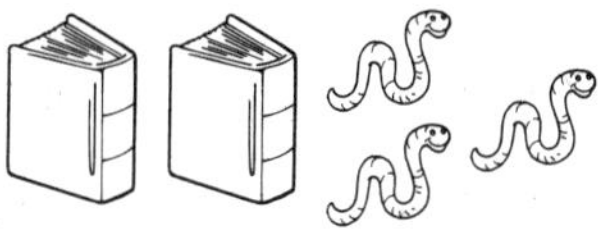

3. If [book][book] 🪱🪱 = 35 lbs. 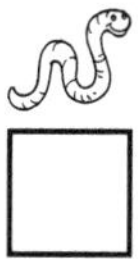   🪱 □ = 35 lbs.

   [book] = _____   🪱 = _____

4. If [book]🪱 = + 2 lbs. = 8 lbs. 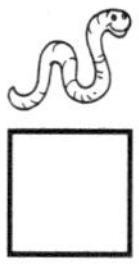   🪱 □ + 2 lbs. = 8 lbs.

   [book] = _____   🪱 = _____

5. If [book]🪱🪱 + 2 lbs. = 22 lbs. 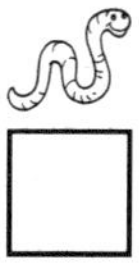   🪱 □ + 2 lbs. = 22 lbs.

   [book] = _____   🪱 = _____

ESTIMATING AND FINDING MASS

Unit 2

Ounces
Estimating
Measuring
Problem solving
Addition
Money
Calculators

Objectives

- *orders whole numbers up to 999*
- *sorts and describes objects in terms of their features such as size and shape*
- *uses materials and models to develop understanding*
- *compares and orders length, capacity and mass in common standard units*
- *uses number skills involving whole numbers to solve problems*
- *appreciates the impact of mathematical information on daily life*
- *uses available technology to help in the solution of mathematical problems*
- *uses one or more strategies to solve mathematical problems*

Language

smallest mass, biggest mass, masses, less, more, estimate, balance, short form, ounce, pound, much heavier, total mass

Materials/Resources

colored pencils, pencils, screws, dimes, Base 10 materials (centicubes/unit cubes), pebbles, supermarket catalogues, scales

Contents of Student Pages

* *Materials needed for each reproducible page*

Page 60 Measuring Mass
Estimating and finding different gram masses; ordering masses.

* *pencils, screws, dimes, Base 10 materials, pebbles, scales*

Page 61 Finding Masses
Adding masses to find total mass.

Page 62 Comparing Masses
Writing mass in short form; working out mass problems from a pictorial chart; finding masses in catalogues.

* *supermarket catalogues*

Page 63 Mass Word Problems
Finding ounce costs from 1lb. prices.

Page 64 Assessment
* *colored pencils*

Remember

❑ *It is important to reinforce that the size of an object does not necessarily give an indication of its mass.*

❑ *Measuring is a hands-on experience. Allow plenty of time for slow workers.*

Additional Activities

❑ *Investigate, using the balance scales, the mass of everyday items (e.g. an orange) when compared with combinations of masses. Encourage hefting before measuring.*

❑ *Allow students to make masses, by putting sand into bags or plastic containers until they balance with the standard masses. Students can use these when estimating by hefting and checking the mass of objects.*

❑ *Provide opportunities for students to measure the mass of packets full and empty and the contents, (example: cardboard packets of pasta). Is there a difference?*

❑ *Discuss why some food items are sold in ounces and others in pounds.*

❑ *Encourage students to look up reference books or appropriate computer sources to find ounce weights of items. Share findings with the class.*

❑ *Do lots of cooking with the students to increase their understanding of ounces. Have them estimate first before measuring masses.*

❑ *Investigate with the class the effect of gravity on mass. Find out what happens to our weight on the moon.*

Answers

Page 60 Measuring Mass

1. Teacher to check.
2. a. Less than 10 oz.: Cheese, Cereal, Pears, Honey, Salt more than 10 oz., but less than 1 lb.: Brown Lentils, Tomato Soup, Baked Beans, Tomato Purée from 1 lb. to 24 oz. Laundry Detergent, Soy Beans, Pasta 24 oz. or more: Diswasher Powder, Peaches, Fruit Cocktail
   b. dishwasher powder
   c. Salt

Page 61 Finding Masses

1. a. 30 oz.
   b. 42 oz.
   c. 20 oz.
   d. 13 oz.
2. a. 24 oz.
   b. 12 oz.
   c. 22 oz.
   d. 22 oz.
   e. 25 oz.
   f. grapes, orange
   g. kiwi fruit, passion fruit
3. a. 30 oz.
   b. 22.5 oz.
   c. 24 oz.
   d. 31 oz.
   e. 21.5 oz.

f. 25 oz.
g. 16.5 oz.
h. 23.5 oz.

Page 62 Comparing Masses

1. a. 300 oz.
   b. 6 oz.
   c. 1,000 oz.
   d. 30 oz.
   e. 500 oz.
   f. 4 lbs.
   g. 430 oz.
   h. 504 oz.
2. a. butter
   b. 125 oz.
   c. 117 oz.
   d. 3 oz.
   e. 108 oz.
   f. 290 oz. (18 lbs. 2 oz.)
3. Teacher to check.

Page 63 Mass Word Problems

1. a. $2.75
   b. 270 lbs.
   c. $2.50, $1.25, $15
   d. 12
   e. 14 oz.
   f. 133 lbs.
   g. 1 lb. packet
   h. 20
   i. 9 oz.
2. Teacher to check.

Page 64 Assessment

1. a. 210 oz.
   b. 794 oz.
   c. 420 oz.
   d. 110 oz.
2. 4, 10, 3, 6, 2, 5, 7, 9, 1, 8
3. Teacher to check.
4. Teacher to check.
5. a. 4
   b. 68 lbs.
   c. 2 oz.
   d. 16 oz. (1 lb.)

59

Name	Date

1. Estimate and then check how many of these items are needed to balance these masses.

Item	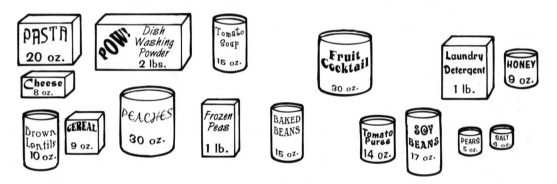 pencil	screw	dime	unit cubes	pebble
Mass	14 oz.	7 oz.	3.5 oz.	10.5 oz.	18 oz.
Estimate					
Check					

2. **a.** Complete the table using these items.

less than 10 oz.	more than 10 oz., but less than 1 lb.	from 1 lb. to 2 lbs.	2 lbs. or more

b. Which item has the greatest mass?_____

c. Which item has the least mass? _____

60

| **Name** | **Date** |

1. What is the total mass of each set of cans?

| **a.** | **b.** | **c.** | **d.** |

baked beans

whole tomatoes

corn kernels

tuna

_____   _____   _____   _____

2.

orange
12 oz.

apple
6 oz.

grapes
11 oz.

kiwi fruit
4 oz.

passion fruit
7 oz.

Find the mass of:

   a. 2 oranges _____

   b. 2 apples _____

   c. 2 bunches of grapes _____

   d. 1 kiwifruit, 1 passion fruit, 1 bunch of grapes _____

   e. 1 orange, 1 apple, 1 passion fruit _____

   f. Choose two pieces of fruit that would give the greatest total mass. _____

   g. Choose two pieces of fruit that would give the least total mass. _____

3.

9 oz.   16 oz.   14 oz.   7.5 oz.   15 oz.

What is the mass of:

   a. pasta and jam? _____   **b.** salmon and cookies? _____

   c. chocolates and cookies? _____   **d.** pasta and cookies? _____

   e. salmon and jam? _____   **f.** chocolates and pasta? _____

   g. salmon and chocolates? _____   **h.** pasta and salmon? _____

61

Name	**Date**

1. Use the short form to write:

   a. three hundred ounces _____ **b.** six ounces _____

   c. one thousand ounces _____ **d.** thirty ounces _____

   e. five hundred ounces _____ **f.** four pounds _____

   g. four hundred and thirty ounces _____

   h. five hundred and four ounces _____

2.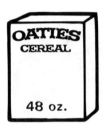

   a. Which item has the greatest mass?_____

   b. What is the total mass of the butter and the pasta? _____

   c. What is the total mass of the jam and the peaches? _____

   d. How much heavier is the butter than the peaches? _____

   e. What is the total mass of the pasta and the cereal? _____

   f. What is the total mass of all the items?_____

3. Look at supermarket catalogues and make a list of items sold in ounces.

Item	Mass	Item	Mass

Name	**Date**

> **Remember:**
> **16 oz. = 1 lb.**

1. Solve these problems. Show all work.

   a. Naseem bought 4 oz. of sliced ham at the delicatessen. If the ham was priced at $11.00 per pound, how much did Naseem pay?

   b. Carlie, Libby and Cassie have masses of 80 lbs., 119 lbs., and 71 lbs. What is their total mass?

   c. King's chocolates cost $5 per pound. How much would:

      8 oz. cost? _____

      4 oz. cost? _____

      3 lbs. cost? _____

   d. How many 8 oz. bags of plain flour can be filled from a 6 lb. bag?

   e. A box containing a doll has a mass of 20 oz. The mass of the packaging is 6 oz. What is the doll's mass?

   f. Guy, Chris and Robert have a total mass of 315 pounds. If Guy has a mass of 116 lbs. and Chris a mass of 66 lbs., what is Robert's mass?

   g. Rice can be bought in either a 4 oz. packet costing $2 or a 1 lb. packet costing $7.50. Which is the cheapest way of buying rice?

   h. Kate bought 10 lbs. of lavender. She packed the lavender into 8 oz. bags. How many bags did she pack?

   i. Peter bought 2 lbs. of chocolate. Richard ate 4 oz., Peter ate 6 oz., Karen ate 5 oz., and Lisa ate 8 oz. of chocolates. What is the mass of the chocolates left?

2. Write a mass problem and solve it.

   _____

   _____

   _____

Name	**Date**

1. Write the mass in short form.

   a. two hundred and ten ounces   _____

   b. seven hundred and ninety-four ounces   _____

   c. four hundred and twenty ounces   _____

   d. one hundred and ten ounces   _____

2. Order these masses from smallest to biggest using the numbers 1 – 10.

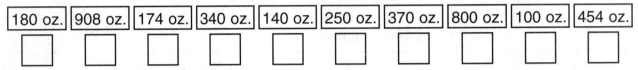

3. Show these masses on the abacus.

   a.   **b.**   **c.**

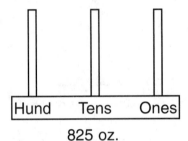
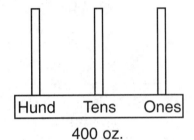

        220 oz.   825 oz.   400 oz.

4. Color the abacus to match.

   a.   **b.**   **c.**   **d.**

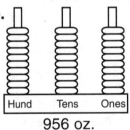
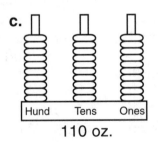
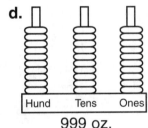

        340 oz.   956 oz.   110 oz.   999 oz.

5. Solve these problems.

   a. How many 8 oz. baskets of strawberries can be filled from a box containing 2 lbs.?

   _____

   b. Alison, Kelly and Anna have a total mass of 286 pounds. If Alison has a mass of 110 lbs., Kelly a mass of 108 lbs., what is Anna's mass?

   _____

   c. A box of candies had a total mass of 1 pound. Pete ate 3 oz., Lisa ate 5 oz., and Paula ate 6 oz.. What is the total mass of candies left?

   _____

   d. A box containing a toy car has a mass of 24 oz. The mass of the packaging is 8 oz. What is the mass of the car?

   _____

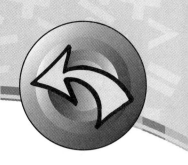

CAPACITY AND VOLUME

These units provide many activities that give students the opportunity to experience capacity and volume in a hands-on way. Students measure with a variety of informal units making use of everyday kitchen containers and progress to formal units using liters and milliliters.

The skills of estimating, comparing and graphing are encouraged. Gallons, fluid ounces, half and quarter liters, graphs using capacity, ordering quantities, writing measurements in short form and measuring in 100 mL quantities all help to consolidate the concepts covered.

There are two assessment pages and one activity page.

© *Teacher Created Resources, Inc.*

#8992 Targeting Math: Measurement

GALLONS, FLUID OUNCES, AND INFORMAL MEASUREMENTS

Unit 1

Informal units
Measuring
Gallon
Fluid Ounce
Ordering capacity
Graphing

Objectives

- estimates, compares, and orders the capacity of containers using informal units
- estimates, compares, measures, and records the capacity of containers to the nearest gallon
- recognizes the need for units smaller than a gallon
- identifies and names the measurements that can be made for an object
- records information about the capacity of a range of containers in a table and/or graph

Language

count, measure, find, volume, order, largest, smallest, gallons, fluid ounces, less than, more than, amounts, graph, quantity, half, quarter

Materials/Resources

various sized containers, water, colored pencils, a marked measuring cup, bucket, tablespoons, supermarket catalogs, large saucepan, gallon milk jug

Contents of Student Pages

* Materials needed for each reproducible student page

Page 68 Gallons
Amounts less than 1 gallon; about 1 gallon; more than 1 gallon.

* various containers, gallon milk jug, water, colored pencils

Page 69 Fluid Ounces
Measuring exact amounts.

* various containers, water, marked measuring cup, colored pencils

Page 70 Graphing Results
Tallying results; vertical column graph.

* large saucepan, various containers, water

Page 71 Assessment
* colored pencils

Page 72 Activity Page—Pipelines
Finding how much water is in each pipeline.

Remember

Before starting ensure each student:
- ❏ is encouraged to talk about results with their peers.
- ❏ is reminded about using water safely in the classroom.
- ❏ is reminded to record results neatly.

Additional Activities

- ❏ *Students use milk cartons as measures. Cut a 1 gallon jug in half to make two 64 ounce containers.*

- ❏ *Students fill 4 clear measuring cups to different levels. Use water that has had food coloring added to show measure clearly. Order the measuring cups from smallest to largest.*

- ❏ *Use solid objects to experiment with volume and capacity. Example: How many baked bean cans will fit into a backpack? How many spoons will fit into a shoe box?*

- ❏ *Students could do a class survey about how much fluid each student drinks over the period of one day. These results are then discussed. A class graph is drawn and displayed.*

Answers

Page 68 Gallons
1. Teacher to check.
2. Less than 1 gallon: lunch box, teacup, eggcup, frying pan, small milk carton
   About 1 gallon: large mixing bowl, large ice-cream container, saucepan
   More than 1 gallon: bucket

Page 69 Fluid Ounces
Teacher to check.

Page 70 Graphing Results
Teacher to check.

Page 71 Assessment
1. a-d. Teacher to check.
   e. c
2. a. ice-cream container, saucepan, large mixing bowl
   b. 3, 4, 1, 2, 8, 5, 6, 7
3. Less than 1 gallon: an eggcup, a teaspoon, a dog's bowl; About 1 gallon: a baby's bath; More than 1 gallon: a bucket, a bathtub

Page 72 Activity Page—Pipelines
a. 341 fl. oz. (2 gal. 85 fl. oz.)
b. 986 fl. oz. (7 gal. 90 fl. oz.)
c. 2, 017 fl. oz. (15 gal. 97 fl. oz.)
   color C

Name	Date

$$\boxed{\textbf{1 gallon (gal.) = 128 fluid ounces (fl. oz.)}}$$

1. Color the measuring cups to match the amounts below.

    a.   **b.**   **c.**

	a. 1 gal.	b. 64 fl. oz.	c. 32 fl. oz.
96 fl. oz.			
64 fl. oz.			
32 fl. oz.			

2. Do the containers below hold about 1 gallon, less than 1 gallon or more than 1 gallon? Use a gallon milk jug to check your results. Check the correct box.

	Container	Less than 1 gallon	About 1 gallon	More than 1 gallon
a.	large mixing bowl			
b.	large ice-cream container			
c.	lunch box			
d.	teacup			
e.	bucket			
f.	saucepan			
g.	eggcup			
h.	frying pan			
i.	small milk carton			

Name	**Date**

1. Color each section in a different color. The first one has been done for you.

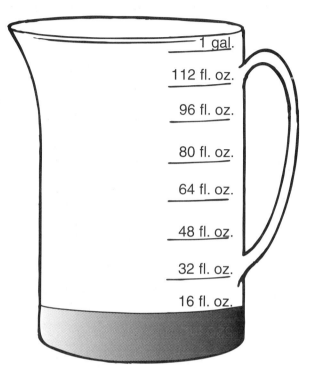

2. Fill each of the containers below with water, then pour that amount into a marked measuring cup. Record your results in the table below.

	Container	Estimate	Actual Measurement
a.	coffee mug		
b.	a jam jar		
c.	a soup ladle		
d.	three tea cups		
e.	a margarine container		
f.	a small cake tin		
g.	an empty vase		

69

Name	Date

1. Fill a large saucepan with water using containers similar to the ones below. Use the tally method to count how many times each container is emptied to fill the saucepan.

	Container	Tally	Total
a.			
b.			
c.			
d.			
e.			

2. Show your results on the vertical column graph. Circle the container that had the smallest volume.

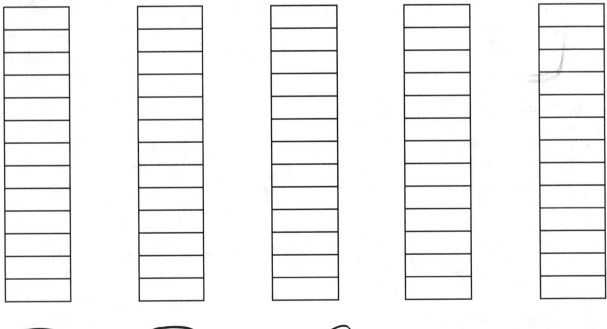

Name	**Date**

1. Color these measuring cups so that they match the amounts.

a.

1 gallon

b.

64 fl. oz.

c.

32 fl. oz.

d.

16 fl. oz.

e. Put a circle around the measuring cup with the smallest amount of water.

2. a. Color the containers blue that would hold about 1 gallon of fluid.

b. Number the above containers from 1 to 8 in order of smallest to largest capacity.

3. Do the containers below hold about 1 gallon, less than 1 gallon or more than 1 gallon? Check the box to show your answer.

Container	Less than 1 gallon	About 1 gallon	More than 1 gallon
a bucket			
an eggcup			
a teaspoon			
a baby's bath			
a bathtub			
a dog's bowl			

71

Name	Date

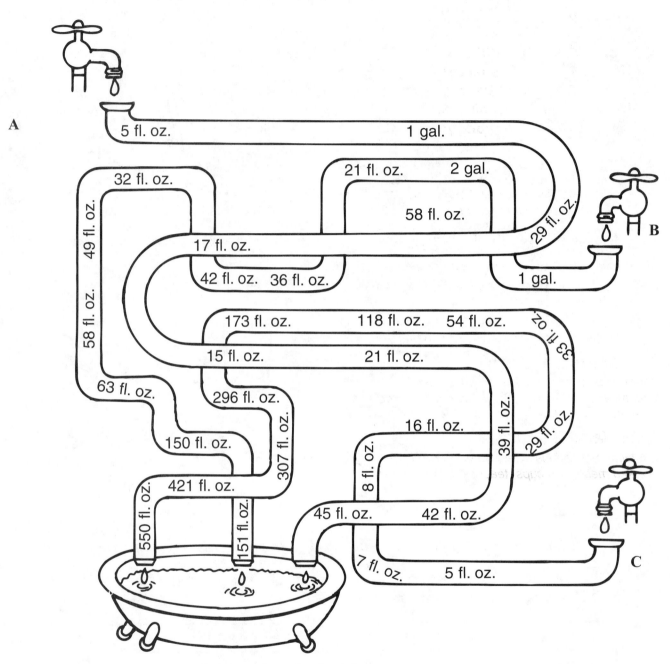

A

5 fl. oz.   1 gal.

21 fl. oz.   2 gal.

32 fl. oz.

58 fl. oz.

49 fl. oz.

17 fl. oz.

29 fl. oz.

B

58 fl. oz.

42 fl. oz.   36 fl. oz.

1 gal.

173 fl. oz.   118 fl. oz.   54 fl. oz.

33 fl. oz.

15 fl. oz.   21 fl. oz.

63 fl. oz.

296 fl. oz.

29 fl. oz.

16 fl. oz.

39 fl. oz.

150 fl. oz.

307 fl. oz.

8 fl. oz.

550 fl. oz.   421 fl. oz.

151 fl. oz.

45 fl. oz.   42 fl. oz.

C

7 fl. oz.   5 fl. oz.

How much water from each tap goes into the bath?

a. _____

b. _____

c. _____

Color the pipe that pours the most water.

72

LITERS AND MILLILITERS

Unit 2

Liters
Milliliters
Measuring
Ordering capacity
Short form
Graphing

Objectives

- estimates, compares, and orders the capacity of containers using informal units
- estimates, compares, measures and records the capacity of containers to the nearest liter
- recognizes the need for units smaller than a liter
- identifies and names the measurements that can be made for an object
- records information about the capacity of a range of containers in a table and/or graph

Language

count, measure, find, volume, order, largest, smallest, liter, milliliters, less than, more than, amounts, graph, quantity, half, quarter

Materials/Resources

containers of various sizes, water, colored pencils, marked measuring cups, teacups, 2-liter soda bottles

Contents of Student Pages

- * *Materials needed for each reproducible student page*

Page 75 Measuring in Liters
Using a 2-liter soda bottle; looking at 100 mL selections.

- * *empty 2-liter soda bottles, measuring cups, water, colored pencils.*

Page 76 Measuring Cups
Calculating quantities; problem solving.

- * *colored pencils*

Page 77 Graphing
Using a teacup as a standard measure; horizontal column graph.

- * *containers, teacups, water*

Page 78 Quantities
True or false; drawing objects; adding quantities; sizing capacities.

Page 79 Assessment

Remember

Before starting ensure each student:
- ❏ is encouraged to talk about results with their peers.
- ❏ is reminded about using water safely in the classroom.
- ❏ is reminded to record results neatly.
- ❏ reads problem solving questions carefully.

(73)

Additional Activities

❑ *Students can take part in cooking lessons. This will provide an opportunity for them to practice measuring various amounts and working with liquids and solids, for example, milk and flour.*

❑ *Students can play guessing games. How many candies in the jar? How many marbles will fit into a shoebox?*

❑ *Collect 1 L, 2 L, 3 L, 4 L and 5 L containers. Observe and discuss the visual change in size as well as the amount of fluid needed to fill each one.*

Answers

Page 75 Measuring in Liters
1. Teacher to check.
2. Teacher to check.

Page 76 Measuring Cups
1. a. 300 mL
   b. 500 mL
   c. 250 mL
   d. 550 mL
   e. 1 mL
   f. 4 mL
   g. 3 mL
   h. 5 mL
2. Teacher to check.
3. a. 200 mL
   b. 580 mL
   c. 6 L 750 mL

Page 77 Graphing
Teacher to check.

Page 78 Quantities
1. a. false
   b. true
   c. true
   d. false
   e. true
2. Teacher to check.
3. a. 6 L 870 mL
   b. 3 L 870 mL
   c. 9 L
   d. 6L 650 mL
   e. 11 L 970 mL
   f. 11 L
   g. 8 L 750 mL
   h. 5 L 860 mL
4. a thimble, an eggcup, soft drink can, a cereal bowl, ice-cream container, a plastic grocery bag, a bucket, a trash can

Page 79 Assessment
1. a. 450 mL
   b. 150 mL
   c. 600 mL
   d. 300 mL
2. a. 650 mL
   b. 4 L 695 mL
   c. 1 L 375 mL
   d. 2 L 642 mL
   e. 5 L 250 mL
   f. 6 L 666 mL
   g. 4 L 565 mL
   h. 7 L 350 mL
3. 650 mL, 1 L 375 mL, 2 L 642 mL, 4 L 565 mL, 4 L 695 mL, 5 L 250 mL, 6 L 666 mL, 7L 350 mL
4. a. 10 L
   b. 250 mL
   c. 1 L
   d. 20 mL
   e. 6 L
   f. 10 mL
   g. 750 mL
   h. 2 L

#8992 Targeting Math: Measurement

Name	**Date**

$$\boxed{\textbf{1 Liter (L) = 1,000 milliliters (mL)}}$$

1. Use a 2–liter soda bottle and find out how many times each container can be filled from it. Record your results.

2. Label each 100 milliliters on the measuring jug. Color each 100 mL a different color.

100 mL

⑦⑤

Name	Date

1. Look at the measuring containers and write how many mL are in each one.

a.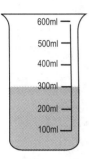

b.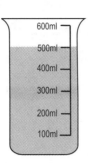

c.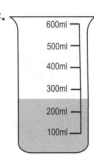

d.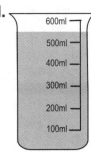

_____ _____ _____ _____

e.

f.

g.

h.

_____ _____ _____ _____

2. Color the measuring containers to show the given amount.

a.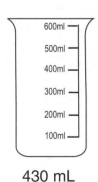

b.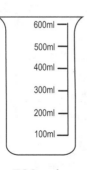

c.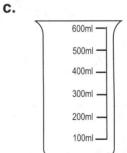

d.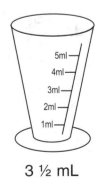

430 mL   520 mL   180 mL   3 ½ mL

3. **a.** If Penny had to take 20 mL of medicine each day for 10 days how many mL did she take altogether? _____

b. If 420 mL were poured out of a 1–liter container, how much would be left? _____

c. 3 containers were filled with water. Each container held 2 L 250 mL. How much water was needed altogether? _____

76

Name	Date

1. Use a teacup to fill each of the containers below. Record how many cupfuls were needed.

	Container	Tally	Total
a.			
b.			
c.			
d.			
e.			

2. Graph the results on the horizontal column graph.

a.

b.

c.

d.

e.

Key ☐ = 1

3. **a.** Which container had the greatest capacity? _____

    b. Which container had the smallest capacity? _____

#8992 Targeting Math: Measurement

Name	**Date**

1. Write true or false for the following statements:

   a. 550 mL is equal to half a liter.   _____

   b. 1 L equals 1,000 mL.   _____

   c. 250 mL equals one quarter of a liter.   _____

   d. 2 L 350 mL < 2 L 250 mL.   _____

   e. 5,698 mL > 4 L 895 mL.   _____

2. Draw two containers that hold about:

   a. half a liter (500 mL)   **b.** a quarter of a liter (250 mL)

3. Add these amounts.

   a. 5 L 650 mL + 1 L 220 mL = _____   **b.** 1 L 670 mL + 2 L 200 mL = _____

   c. 8 L 120 mL + 880 mL =   _____   **d.** 5 L 900 mL + 750 mL =   _____

   e. 9 L 630 mL + 2 L 340 mL = _____   **f.** 10 L 250 mL + 750 mL =   _____

   g. 6 L 750 mL + 2 L =   _____   **h.** 2 L 360 mL + 3 L 500 mL = _____

4. List these containers from smallest to largest capacity.

   an ice-cream container, a soft drink can, a cereal bowl, a thimble, an eggcup, a trash can, a bucket and a plastic grocery bag.

   _____

   _____

   _____

78

Name	**Date**

1. Look at the measuring containers and write how many milliliters are in each one.

a. 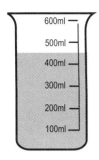   **b.** 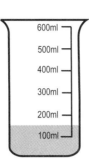   **c.** 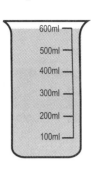   **d.**

_____   _____   _____   _____

2. Write these amounts in short form. Use L and mL.

   a. 650 milliliters =   _____   **b.** 4,695 milliliters =   _____

   c. 1 liter and 375 milliliters =   _____   **d.** 2,642 milliliters =   _____

   e. 5 liters and 250 milliliters = _____   **f.** 6,666 milliliters =   _____

   g. 4,565 milliliters =   _____   **h.** 7 liters 350 milliliters =   _____

3. Write the above amounts in order from smallest to largest capacity.

_____, _____, _____, _____

_____, _____, _____, _____

4. Write mL or L next to each quantity to show the correct capacity.

   a.    **b.**    **c.**    **d.**

   10 _____   250 _____   1 _____   20 _____

   e.    **f.**   **g.**   **h.**

   6 _____   10 _____   750 _____   2 _____

79

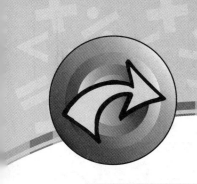

ANGLES

The emphasis of the angle unit is to identify angles and using everyday language, then use the correct terminology to describe them.

Skills include drawing, comparing, ordering, and matching angles less than 180 degrees.

One assessment page has been included.

#8992 Targeting Math: Measurement

RIGHT, ACUTE, AND OBTUSE ANGLES

Unit 1

Right
Acute
Obtuse angles
Ordering

Objectives

- makes sensible estimates based on provided units
- uses indirect methods to order angles
- identifies angles
- identifies and orders angles using direct comparison
- chooses an appropriate uniform unit when measuring
- describes and compares angles using everyday language

Language

greater than, smaller than, straight, obtuse, acute, right angle 90°, sides, angles

Materials/Resources

scrap paper, ruler, colored pencils, protractor

Contents of Student Pages

* Materials needed for each reproducible student page

Page 83 Acute and Obtuse Angles
Using these terms to identify and group angles; matching angles.

Page 84 Drawing Angles
Drawing acute and obtuse angles; identifying angles in shapes.

* colored pencils

Page 85 Right Angles
Identifying right angles.

* scrap paper

Page 86 Ordering Angles
Placing angles in the correct order from smallest to largest and largest to smallest.

* protractor (optional)

Page 87 Drawing Shapes with Angles
Finishing shapes from angles and identifying the number of sides and angles.

* colored pencils, ruler

Page 88: Assessment
* colored pencils

Remember

Remind students to:
- ❏ always use a ruler to draw angles.
- ❏ use a sharp pencil when drawing angles.

Additional Activities

❑ Students put themselves in groups of eight. Using their bodies, lying down on the floor they create each of the following angles; acute, obtuse, straight and right.

❑ Interview a builder, architect or a carpenter and ask them what instruments they use to make angles, and why angles might be important in their jobs.

❑ Write down all the upper case letters in the alphabet. Underneath each one write how many angles are in each letter.

Example:

     C   Z   T

no angle   2 angles   2 angles

❑ Using a variety of colored strips of paper, create patterns with angles.

Answers

Page 83 Acute and Obtuse Angles
1. a. A
   b. O
   c. O
   d. A
   e. A
   f. A
   g. A
   h. O
   i. O
   j. O
   k. O
   l. A
2. Teacher to check.

Page 84 Drawing Angles
1. Teacher to check.
2. Teacher to check.
3. Teacher to check.

Page 85 Right Angles
1. a and f are right angles
2. Teacher to check.
3. Teacher to check.
4. Teacher to check.

Page 86 Ordering Angles
1. From left to right 4, 2, 3, 1, 5
2. From left to right 4, 3, 1, 2, 5
3. Angles that should be circled: b, c, d, i.

Page 87 Drawing Shapes with Angles
1. Teacher to check.
2. Student should draw a comparison that the number of angles is equal to the number of sides.

Page 88 Assessment
1. a. acute
   b. obtuse
   c. obtuse
   d. acute
2. a. acute
   b. acute
   c. obtuse
   d. acute
3. angles that are checked: a, c
4. a. acute
   b. obtuse
   c. right
   d. straight
5. Teacher to check.

Name	**Date**

Angles that are smaller than 90° are called **acute** angles.
Angles that are bigger than 90° are called **obtuse** angles.
Angles that are exactly 90° are called **right** angles.
Lines that have no angles are called **straight** angles.

1. Place "a" for acute or "o" for obtuse on each of these angles.

a.  **b.** 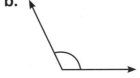 **c.**  **d.**

e.   **f.**  **g.**  **h.**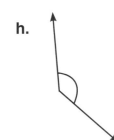

i. 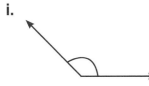 **j.**  **k.**  **l.**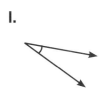

2. Match pairs of angles that are the same by drawing a line between matching angles. Find acute, obtuse, right and straight angles.

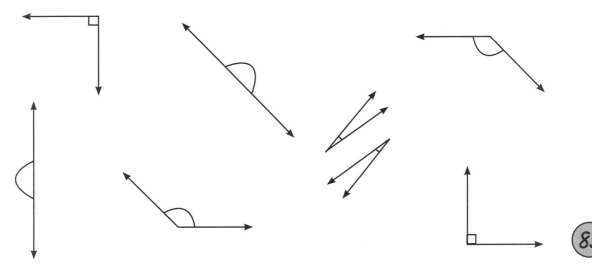

Name	**Date**

1. Look at each of these angles. Draw another angle that is smaller, or more acute.

   a. 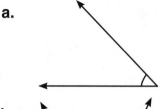   new angle ⟶

   b. 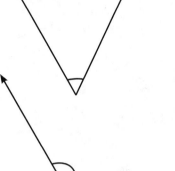   new angle ⟶

   c. 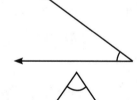   new angle ⟶

2. Look at each of these angles. Draw another angle that is larger, or more obtuse.

   a.    new angle ⟶

   b.    new angle ⟶

   c.   new angle ⟶

3. Look at each of these shapes. Place a colored dot on all the angles.

84

Name	**Date**

These are all right angles.

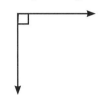 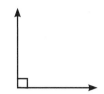 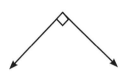 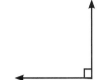

1. Tear off the corner from a piece of scrap paper and use it to test if these angles are right angles. Draw in the corner symbol if the angle is a right angle.

a. 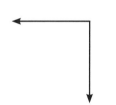   **b.** 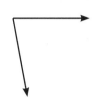   **c.** 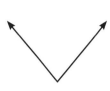   **d.**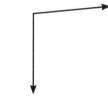

e.    **f.**    **g.**   **h.**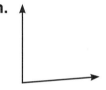

2. List 5 objects that have right angles in your classroom.

_____   _____   _____

_____   _____

3. List 5 objects that have acute angles in your classroom.

_____   _____   _____

_____   _____

4. List 5 objects that have no angles in your classroom.

_____   _____   _____

_____   _____

85

Name	**Date**

1. Order these angles from greatest (most obtuse) to smallest (most acute). Use the numbers 1 to 5. You may need to use a protractor.

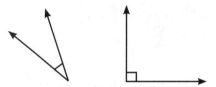 

2. Order these angles from smallest (most acute) to greatest (most obtuse). Use the numbers 1 to 5. You may need to use a protractor.

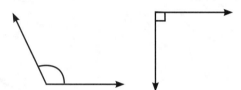 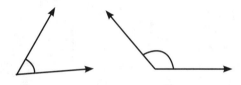

3. Right angles are equal to 90. Circle the angles that are less than 90.

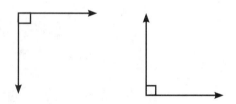

a.   **b.**   **c.**

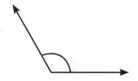

d.   **e.**   **f.**

g.   **h.**   **i.**

 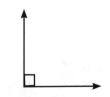

86

Name	**Date**

1. Using a colored pencil and a ruler change these angles into shapes. You may use as many straight lines as you like.

   Follow this example: List how many sides and angles your new shape has.

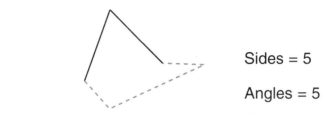

Sides = 5

Angles = 5

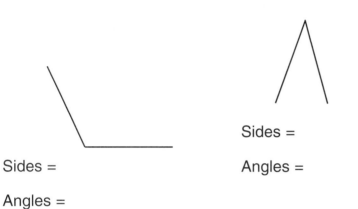

Sides =

Angles =

Sides =

Angles =

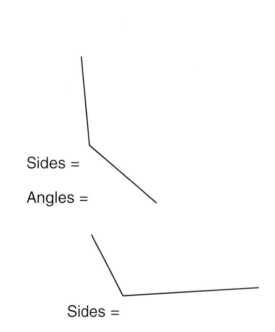

Sides =

Angles =

Sides =

Angles =

Sides =

Angles =

Sides =

Angles =

Sides =

Angles =

2. Can you write a sentence about the number of sides and the number of angles for one of your shapes?

_____

_____

_____

87

Name	Date

1. Label these angles acute or obtuse.

   a.   **b.**    **c.**    **d.**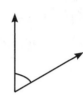

2. Label these angles obtuse or acute.

   a.   **b.**   **c.**    **d.**

3. Identify with a √ which of these angles are right angles.

   a.    **b.**   **c.** 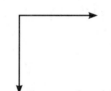   **d.**

4. Fill in the missing words.

   a. An angle that is less than 90° is called an <u>a</u>_____ angle.

   b. An angle that is greater than 90° is called an <u>o</u>_____ angle.

   c. A 90° angle is called a <u>r</u>_____ angle.

   d. This is a <u>s</u>_____ angle.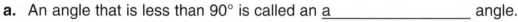

5. Place a colored dot on all of the angles inside these shapes.

     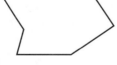

TIME

This section on time contains exercises in identifying parts of hours, revising the concepts of o'clock and half-past and reading and writing time accurately on both digital and analog clocks. A.M. and P.M. times, using a calendar, reading timetables, relating time to everyday experiences and writing time in words are all used to practice skills.

Students draw on their knowledge to extract information from timetables, calculate small time intervals and relate time to everyday situations.

There are two assessment pages included and three activity pages.

WRITING TIME

Unit 1

O'clock
Half hours
Quarter hours
Minutes
Writing time
Facts

Objectives

- understands the concept of half past and o'clock
- demonstrates time in quarter of an hour intervals
- tells time on both analog and digital clocks
- reads and writes time in minute intervals
- writes time in numerals and words
- demonstrates an awareness of time and seasons
- orders seasons and months

Language

minute, hour, second, calendar, o'clock, half past, digital, analog, quarter to (the hour), quarter past (the hour), A.M., P.M.

Materials/Resources

colored pencils, reference books or internet access

Contents of Student Pages

* Materials needed for each reproducible student page

Page 92 O' Clock and Half Past
Revising time - o'clock; half past.

Page 93 Quarter Past, Quarter to
Identifying quarter past and quarter to the hour; analog and digital time.
* colored pencils

Page 94 Minutes Past, Minutes To
Time in 5 minute intervals; rewriting analog and digital time.

Page 95 Minutes Past
More minutes past - identifying time in minute intervals.
* colored pencils

Page 96 Writing Time
Expressing time in numerals and words; in digital and analog form.

Page 97 Time Facts
Time; months; seasons; days.
* reference books or internet access

Page 98 Assessment
Page 99: Activity Page—New Calendar
Making a different calendar.

Remember

❑ Make sure each student knows the difference between analog and digital clock faces.

Additional Activities

❑ At home the student walks around their house and lists every household item that uses a clock. Example: microwave oven.

❑ As a class or a small group research the instruments in history that have been used to measure time, for example, water clocks and sundials.

❑ Create a class book containing jokes about time.

❑ Using a calendar, work out how many minutes/days you have been alive, from 8:00 A.M. on the day you were born to 8:00 A.M. on the present day.

❑ Survey 20 people to find out their favorite season of the year. Graph your results on a picture graph.

Answers

Page 92 O 'Clock and Half Past
1. a. 3 o'clock; 3:00
   b. 6 o'clock; 6:00
   c. 9 o'clock; 9:00
   d. 12 o'clock; 12:00
2. Teacher to check drawings.
   a. 7:30
   b. 2:30
   c. 10:30
   d. 6:30
3. a. six o'clock
   b. nine o'clock
   c. half past six
   d. half past ten
   e. four o'clock
   f. half past twelve
4. Teacher to check.

Page 93 Quarter Past, Quarter To
1. a. 7:15   c. 9:45   e. 9:15   g. 1:45
   b. 3:15   d. 4:45   f. 11:15   h. 11:45
2. Teacher to check.

Page 94 Minutes Past, Minutes To
1. a. Clockwise from 12:00: 10 min. past, 20 past, 25 past, 20 min. to, ¼ to, 10 min. to, 5 min. to
   b. Clockwise from 12:00: :10, :15, :20, :25, :35, :40, :45, :55
2. Teacher to check.
3. a. 6:10
   b. 11:25
   c. 8:45
   d. 11:55
   e. 1:20
   f. 4:15
   g. 3:05
   h. 4:35

Page 95 Minutes Past
1. Teacher to check.
2. Teacher to check.
3. a. 34   f. 2
   b. 44   g. 10
   c. 17   h. 49
   d. 54   i. 29
   e. 21   j. 43

Page 96 Writing Time
1. a. five eleven, 11 past 5
   b. twelve forty-five, 45 past 12
   c. four fifteen, 15 past 4
   d. ten o'clock, 10 o'clock
   e. eight o-five, 5 past 8
   f. two thirty, 30 past 2
2. a. 59 past 2   d. 22 to 4
   b. 8 past 1   e. 15 past 7
   c. 14 to 11
3. Teacher to check.
4. Teacher to check.

Page 97 Time Facts
1. a. 4
   b. Spring, Summer, Autumn, Winter
2. a. 12
   b. February, March, April, June, September, November, December
3. June, July, Aug.; Sept., Oct., Nov.; Dec., Jan., Feb; Mar., Apr., May;
4. a. 365
   b. 366
5. February
6. Every 4 years
7. 52
8. Summer months
9. a. 24 hours
   b. 60, 120, 330

Page 98 Assessment
1. Teacher to check.
2. a. 2:58   b. 10:15
   c. 4:49   d. 9:43
   e. 12:35   f. 7:20
3. a. five eleven; eleven minutes past five
   b. six o'clock
   c. six fifteen; fifteen minutes past six
   d. eight forty-five; fifteen minutes to nine
   e. twelve oh six; six minutes past 12
4. December, November, October, September, August, July, June, May, April, March, February, January
5. a. 30   c. 31   e. 31
   b. 31   d. 31
6. a. 10,080 minutes
   b. 730 days
   c. 3,600 seconds
   d. 60 months
   e. 30 years

Page 99 Activity Page—New Calendar
Teacher to check

Name	Date

1. Write the time shown on each clock in analog and digital time.

a.    **b.** 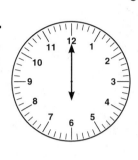   **c.**    **d.**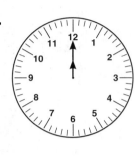

_____ o'clock   _____   _____   _____

[:]   [:]   [:]   [:]

There are 60 minutes in one hour. There are 30 minutes in ½ (half) an hour.

Remember the little hand moves too.

It must be half-way between one hour and the next.

2. Draw the time on these analog clocks.
   Record the time under each clock in digital time.

a.    **b.**    **c.**    **d.**

 ½ past 7   ½ past 2   ½ past 10   ½ past 6

[:]   [:]   [:]   [:]

3. Write these times in words. For example, five o'clock or half past five.

   a. 6:00 _____   **b.** 9:00 _____

   c. 6:30 _____   **d.** 10:30 _____

   e. 4:00 _____   **f.** 12:30 _____

4. **a.** Are you wearing a watch today? _____

   (92) **b.** Is it an analog watch or a digital watch? _____

Name   **Date**

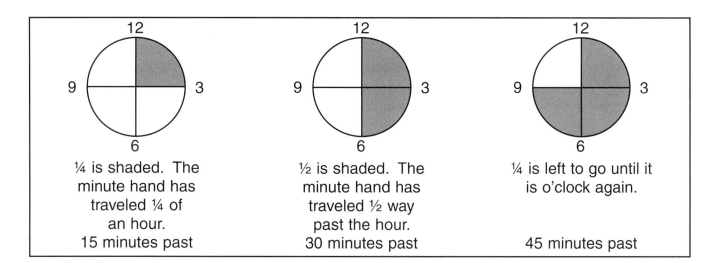

¼ is shaded. The minute hand has traveled ¼ of an hour.
15 minutes past

½ is shaded. The minute hand has traveled ½ way past the hour.
30 minutes past

¼ is left to go until it is o'clock again.

45 minutes past

1. Change these analog times to digital time. Draw the time on the digital watches.

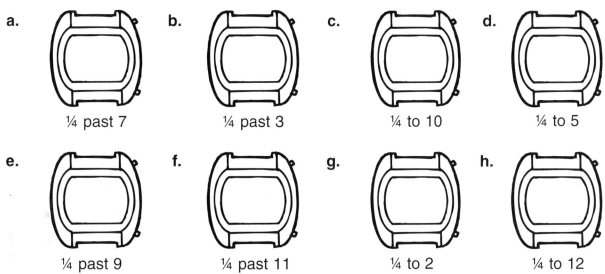

a. ¼ past 7   b. ¼ past 3   c. ¼ to 10   d. ¼ to 5

e. ¼ past 9   f. ¼ past 11   g. ¼ to 2   h. ¼ to 12

2. Draw the time on these analog clocks. Use a color for the hour hand (little hand).

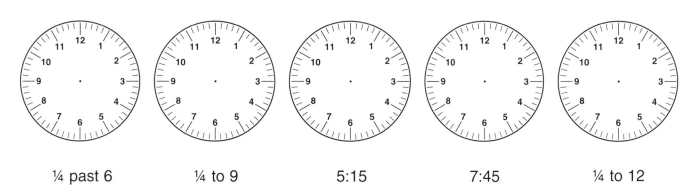

¼ past 6   ¼ to 9   5:15   7:45   ¼ to 12

93

| **Name** | **Date** |

Minutes past the hour 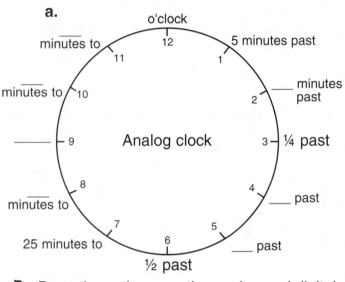   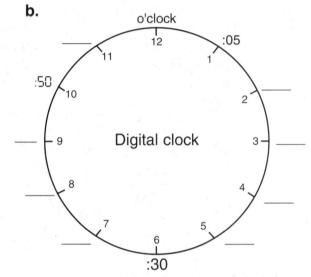 Minutes to the hour

1. Fill in the missing spaces on the clocks below.

a.

o'clock

_____ minutes to   12

5 minutes past

_____ minutes to   10   _____ minutes past

Analog clock   ¼ past

_____ past

_____ minutes to

25 minutes to   _____ past

½ past

b.

o'clock

_____   12   :05

:50   10

Digital clock   _____

_____   9   3   _____

_____ 8   _____

_____   6   _____

:30

2. Draw these times on the analog and digital clock faces.

| **a.** 25 past 6 | **b.** 10 to 9 | **c.** 20 to 8 | **d.** 5 past 7 | **e.** 25 to 1 |

3. Rewrite these analog times as digital times.

a. 10 past 6   [:]   **b.** 25 past 11   [:]   **c.** 15 to 9   [:]

d. 5 to 12   [:]   **e.** 20 past 1   [:]   **f.** 15 past 4   [:]

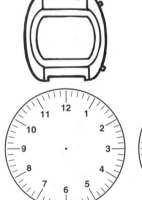 **g.** 5 past 3   [:]   **h.** 25 to 5   [:]

Name	**Date**

1. The watchmaker has forgotten to put the hands on each of these clocks. Can you help him and draw in the missing hand in color?

a.

5 minutes to 6

b.

¼ to 9

c.

26 past 4

d.

¼ past 7

e.

39 minutes past 1

f.

43 minutes past 8

g.

17 minutes to 9

h.

11 minutes to 12

2. Draw the time on these clocks.

a.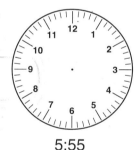

5:55

b.

7:11

c.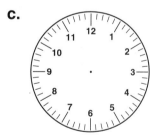

3:49

d.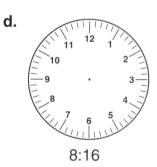

8:16

3. How many minutes more:

   a. from 26 past to the next hour? _____   **b.** from 16 past to the next hour? _____

   c. from 43 past to the next hour? _____   **d.** from 6 past to the next hour? _____

   e. from 39 past to the next hour? _____   **f.** from 58 past to the next hour? _____

   g. from 50 past to the next hour? _____   **h.** from 11 past to the next hour? _____

   i. from 31 past to the next hour? _____   **j.** from 17 past to the next hour? _____

95

Name	**Date**

1. Time can be written in many different ways. Follow the example to fill in the missing spaces below.

Example: 3:26   three twenty-six   26 minutes past 3

   a.   5:11   _____   _____

   b.   12:45   _____   _____

   c.   4:15   _____   _____

   d.   10:00   _____   _____

   e.   8:05   _____   _____

   f.   2:30   _____   _____

2. Fill in the spaces under each digital clock.

a.  **b.**  **c.**  **d.**  **e.**

___ past ___   ___ past ___   ___ past ___   ___ past ___   ___ past ___

3. Look at the numbers on a digital clock face. They are not rounded. Why? _____

_____

_____

4. Change these numbers to ones you would see on a digital clock. Example: 4:26 = 4:26

   a. 3:39 = _____   **b.** 12:01 = _____

   c. 10:36 = _____   **d.** 7:58 = _____

   e. 11:07 = _____   **f.** 8:40 = _____

   g. 5:55 = _____   **h.** 4:03 = _____

Put an X next to the one that was the hardest to write.
Put a √ next to the one that was easiest to write.

#8992 Targeting Math: Measurement   © *Teacher Created Resources, Inc.*

Name	**Date**

You may look up the answers to these questions in reference books or on the Internet.

1. **a.** How many seasons in one year?_____

    b. Name them. _____

2. **a.** How many months in a year? _____

    b. Fill in the missing months in order.

    January _____ _____ _____ May _____

    July   August   _____   October   _____   _____

3. Place the months of the year into the correct box.

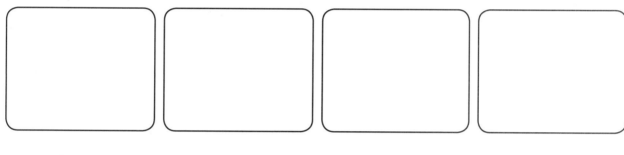

Summer   Autumn   Winter   Spring

4. **a.** How many days in a year?_____

    b. a leap year? _____

5. Which month of the year gets the extra day? _____

6. How often does a leap year occur? _____

7. How many weeks in a year? _____

8. Which months of the year have the longest days? _____

9. **a.** How many hours in a full day? (including the night)_____

    b. How many minutes in: 1 hour? _____, 2 hours? _____, 5 1/2 hours? _____

97

Name	**Date**

1. Draw the time on the analog clocks. Write the time on the digital clocks.

12 o'clock   half past seven   4:25   five o'eight   35 past four

2. Record these times in digital form.

   a. 2 to 3   →   _____   **b.** 15 past 10   →   _____

   c. 11 to 5   →   _____   **d.** 17 to 10   →   _____

   e. 25 to 1   →   _____   **f.** 20 past 7   →   _____

3. Write these times in words. Example: 1:10 one ten; ten minutes past one

   a. 5:11   _____   _____

   b. 6:00   _____   _____

   c. 6:15   _____   _____

   d. 8:45   _____   _____

   e. 12:06   _____   _____

4. Write the months of the year in reverse order.

   December _____

   _____

   _____

5. How many days in the following months?   6. How many:

   a. April   _____   **a.** minutes in one week?   _____

   b. October   _____   **b.** days in 2 non-leap years?   _____

   c. December   _____   **c.** seconds in one hour?   _____

   d. March   _____   **d.** months in 5 years?   _____

   (98) **e.** January   _____   **e.** years in 3 decades?   _____

Name	**Date**

Chief Bulabaloo of the tiny island of Wizzbang decides to hold a competition to design a new calendar. He is tired of the old one! The winner is to have a year's supply of chocolate frogs and strawberry ice cream. You really want to win!

The competition form tells you the rules.

> **There must be an even number of months.**
>
> **Each month's name begins with the letter B.**
>
> **Each week will be 8 days long and there will be three-day weekends.**
>
> **Each day's name begins with the letter W.**
>
> **You must show two months of your calendar on your entry.**
>
> **You must write all the names of the months and days.**

You decide to work with a friend and to share the prize if you win. (Hint: Remember that there are 365 days in a year.)

Draw and write your winning entry below.

READING AND ORDERING TIME

Unit 2

Ordering time
A.M. or P.M.
Calendars
Timetable
Stopwatch

Objectives

- orders time in hour and minutes intervals
- demonstrates the concept of A.M. and P.M.
- uses a calendar to describe day and date
- relates time to everyday activities
- measures small intervals of time using a stopwatch
- reads and interprets timetables

Language

A.M., P.M., estimate, decade, analog, digital

Materials/Resources

Stopwatch

Contents of Student Pages

Remember

❑ Make sure students are aware of difference between analog and digital clocks.
❑ Review short, hour hand, long, minute hand.

Additional Activities

❏ *Write out a timetable of activities that you do in a day, including breaks in your school day. Use digital time to record your activities. Example: 6:00 a.m. Got out of bed.*

❏ *Survey 20 people and find out if they are/are not in favor of daylight savings. Record your results on a picture graph.*

❏ *Make a list of 7 professions that rely heavily on time. Example: an anesthetist - the amount of drug used depends on the time the patient must stay asleep during an operation.*

❏ *Estimating game: Teacher asks students to estimate when they think a minute has passed. They can stand or sit when they think the time is up.*

❏ *Students write acronyms for the months of the year.*

Answers
Page 102 Ordering Time
From bottom to top:

1:00, 1:13, 2:27, 2:54, 3:00, 3:15, 3:40, ¼ to 4, 5:05, 5:10, 6:01, 6:16, 6:45, 7:00

  a. 6 hours   d. 9 and 10
  b. 6 minutes   e. 3:40
  c. 10 and 11   f. 5:10, Teacher to check drawing.

Page 103 A.M. and P.M.
1. a. P.M.   f. P.M.
   b. A.M.   g. A.M.
   c. P.M.   h. A.M.
   d. P.M.   i. A.M.
   e. P.M.   j. P.M.
2. a. 7:00 A.M.   e. 1:15 A.M.
   b. 6:30 P.M.   f. 2:45 P.M.
   c. 8:45 P.M.   g. 11:59 A.M.
   d. 3:23 P.M.   h. 12:01 A.M.
3. a. 9:24 A.M.   e. 1:29 P.M.
   b. 12:56 A.M.   f. 12:13 P.M.
   c. 3:41 A.M.   g. 6:17 P.M.
   d. 2:01 P.M.   h. 10:35 A.M.
4. Teacher to check.

Page 104 Using a Calendar
1. September, teacher to check dates
2. August, November
3. a. Friday   e. Saturday
   b. Sunday   f. Saturday
   c. Wednesday g. Monday
   d. Thursday   h. Tuesday
4. 9
5. October
6. 5
7. 22
8. a. 29   b. 366
9. 6
10. Teacher to check.

Page 105 Working with Time

1. a. brushing your teeth
   b. turning out the light
   c. answering the telephone
   d. eating your dinner
   e. getting dressed
   f. boiling water
2. a. F   d. T
   b. T   e. F
   c. F
3. Teacher to check.
4. a. 8:00   d. 6:00 P.M.
   b. 11:59   e. 140 min.
   c. 6:30 P.M.   f. Teacher to check.

Page 106 Minutes More
1. Teacher to check.
2. a. 13 min.   c. 35 min. e. 0 min. g. 6 hours
   b. 1 hr. 4 min. d. 30 min. f. 8 min. h. 4 hours

Page 107 Reading a Timetable
1. a. 2 min.   f. 1 hr. 55 min.
   b. Forest walk   g. 55 min.
   c. Tidying   h. putting slippers on and
   d. 1 hour   walking to the kitchen
   e. Drinking tea   i. 1 hr. 28 min.
                j. 1 min.
                k. 385 min. or 6 hr. 25 min.

Page 108 Assessment
1. a. 3:03 A.M., 3:13 A.M., 2:24 P.M., 7:05 P.M.
   b. 6 o'clock A.M., 8 o'clock A.M., 6 o'clock P.M., 8 o'clock P.M.
   c. 11 past 3, 26 past 3, 27 past 3, 38 past 3
   d. ½ past 3, ¼ to 4, ¼ past 4, ½ past 4
2. a. 4:24   d. 12:51 g. 6:55
   b. 5:46   e. 3:11   h. 9:25
   c. 10:18   f. 1:10
3. a. 200   c. Mon.
   b. 61   d. January 1, 2000
4. Teacher to check.
5. Teacher to check.
6. a. 3 hours   d. 2 centuries
   b. ¾ min.   e. 1 ½ days
   c. 2 years   f. 7 months

Page 109 Activity Page—Interesting Dates
1. 1894   6. 1865
2. 20th century, 2   7. 3, Before Current Era
3. 1971   8. 3,274 years
4. 1819   9. 1641
5. 500 centuries 10. 1812

Page 110 Activity Page—Magic Marshmallows
1. a. 4   d. 512
   b. 32   e. 4,096
   c. 64
2. 1 hr. 10 min.
3. a. 1 hr. 30 min.   c. 1 hr. 35 min.
   b. 1 hr. 25 min.
4. Teacher to check.

Name   **Date**

Look at the times in the 2 boxes.
Place them in the smoke clouds in
the correct ascending order.

a. How long between the first
and the last smoke clouds? _____

b. How many minutes between
smoke cloud 4 and 5? _____

c. Between which two clouds
did the most time elapse? _____

d. Between which two clouds did
the smallest amount of time lapse? _____

e. What time is on the 7th
cloud? Write it in digital time. _____

f. What time is on the 10th cloud?
Draw a clock face to show it. _____

five-oh-five

3 o'clock   6:16   three fifteen

3:40

2:54   7:00

¼ to 4

two twenty-seven   ¼ past 3

ten past 5   six forty-five

1 minute past 6   1:00   1:13

102

Name	**Date**

A.M. stands for Ante Meridiem, which means "before noon." P.M. stands for Post Meridiem, "after noon."

1. Look at the following activities and decide if they would take place in A.M. or P.M. time.

    a. lunch   _____   **b.** morning tea   _____

    c. fireworks display _____   **d.** a midnight snack   _____

    e. homework   _____   **f.** bedtime story   _____

    g. breakfast   _____   **h.** dew falling   _____

    i. sunrise   _____   **j.** nightmare   _____

2. Write these times on the digital clocks. State whether they are A.M. or P.M.

    a. 7 o'clock (morning) _____ [:]   **b.** half past 6 (evening) _____ [:]

    c. quarter to 9 (evening) _____ [:]   **d.** 23 past 3 (afternoon) _____ [:]

    e. quarter past 1 (night) _____ [:]   **f.** 45 past 2 (afternoon) _____ [:]

    g. 1 minute before noon _____ [:]   **h.** 1 minute after midnight _____ [:]

3. Add 2 hours to each of these times. Change the A.M. or P.M. if necessary.

    a. 7:24 A.M.   _____   **b.** 10:56 P.M.   _____

    c. 1:41 A.M.   _____   **d.** 12:01 P.M.   _____

    e. 11:29 A.M.   _____   **f.** 10:13 A.M.   _____

    g. 4:17 P.M.   _____   **h.** 8:35 A.M.   _____

4. Some activities can be done in the morning or afternoon/evening.

    For example, feeding pets or brushing your teeth. Write a list of 6 activities that you can do in either A.M. or P.M. time.

    _____   _____

    _____   _____

    _____   _____

(103)

Name	Date

Sun.	Mon.	Tue.	Wed.	Thur.	Fri.	Sat.
			1		3	4
5			8	9	10	
			15			
19	20	21				
		28				

OCTOBER						
Sun.	Mon.	Tue.	Wed.	Thur.	Fri.	Sat.
						2
10	11					
			20	21		
						30

1. Look at the 2 months. Put in the missing dates and title.

2. Name the months that come before and after these two months.

   _____   _____

3. What day of the week are the following dates.

   a. 1st of October   _____   **b.** 31st of October   _____

   c. 22nd of September _____   **d.** last day of September _____

   e. 9th of October   _____   **f.** 11th of September   _____

   g. 27th of September _____   **h.** 5th of October   _____

4. How many Wednesdays in September and October altogether? _____

5. Which month has the most days? _____

6. How many weekends in October? _____

7. How many weekdays in September? _____

8. If it was a leap year:

   a. How many days would be in February? _____

   b. How many days would be in the year? _____

9. How many months of the year contain the letter "a"? _____

10. Write 2 questions of your own about these two months.

    a. _____

    b. _____

(104)

Name	**Date**

1. Which would be quicker? Circle your choice.

   a. brushing your teeth (or) reading a novel?

   b. walking the dog (or) turning out a light?

   c. doing your homework (or) answering the telephone?

   d. eating your dinner (or) sleeping for 5 hours?

   e. getting dressed (or) doing the supermarket shopping?

   f. boiling water (or) cooking a roast chicken?

2. Write True or False next to these statements.

   a. There are 25 hours in a full day.   _____

   b. A decade is the same as 10 years.   _____

   c. 60 minutes make 60 hours.   _____

   d. 100 years is the same as a century.   _____

   e. A second is longer than a minute.   _____

3. (For this activity you will need a stopwatch.) Estimate how long it will take to do each of these activities. Then time yourself and record your results.

	Est.	Actual
a. walk from your desk to the classroom door	_____	_____
b. spin around 15 times	_____	_____
c. say out loud your 10 times tables	_____	_____
d. tie up your shoelace	_____	_____

4. I'm thinking of a time…

   a. exactly half way between 7 o'clock and 9 o'clock.   _____

   b. one minute before noon.   _____

   c. not one, not two, but one and a half hours after 5 P.M.   _____

   d. 6 o'clock in the morning plus 12 more hours.   _____

   e. the number of minutes between 1:00 and 3:20.   _____

   f. 20 minutes before school starts each day.   _____

(105)

| **Name** | **Date** |

1. Look at the time on the first clock. Follow the instructions and record the new time on the second clock.

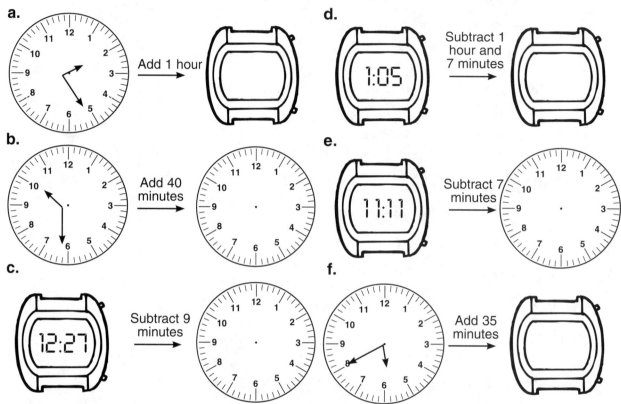

2. Look at these times. How many minutes/hours difference are there?

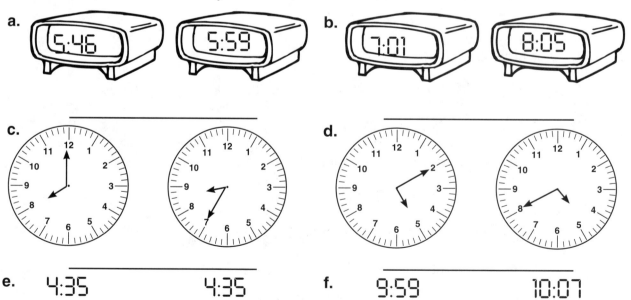

e. 4:35   4:35

f. 9:59   10:07

g. half past 1   half past 7

h. 15 minutes to 3   15 minutes to 7

Name	**Date**

A Goblin's Daily Timetable

6:10	Wake up	12:30	Nap.
6:15	Put slippers on and walk to the kitchen.	1:25	Lunch and play computer games.
		2:15	Read latest, exciting novel.
6:16	Make dandelion tea.	3:06	Collect mail and respond to letter.
6:18	Drink tea and think about the day.	4:11	Relax and drink clover tea.
7:02	Get dressed.	4:21	Do daily exercises.
7:05	Feed pet mice, snakes and spiders; clean cages, etc.	4:31	Prepare dinner and do laundry.
8:05	Go for a walk in forest to collect seeds and mushrooms.	6:05	Watch news on internet.
		7:11	Dinner.
11:16	Return home and tidy up house.	8:11	Lights out.

1. Answer the following questions about the Goblin's daily timetable.

   a. How long does it take to make dandelion tea? _____

   b. Which activity in the morning takes the longest time? _____

   c. What is the goblin doing at noon? _____

   d. How many *hours* does the goblin spend taking care of his pets? _____

   e. What is Goblin doing at 4:15 P.M.? _____

   f. How long is it from waking up until leaving for the forest? _____

   g. How many minutes does Goblin sleep during the day? _____

   h. Which activity requires the least amount of time? _____

   i. How long does Goblin spend drinking tea in total for 2 days? _____

   j. How long does it take him to walk to the kitchen? _____

   k. If Goblin takes a nap every day, how long does he "nap" for in one week? _____

Name	**Date**

1. Order these times from the earliest to the latest.

   a. 2:24 P.M., 3:13 A.M., 7:05 P.M., 3:03 A.M. _____

   b. 6 o'clock A.M., 6 o'clock P.M., 8 o'clock P.M., 8 o'clock A.M. _____

   c. 26 past 3, 38 past 3, 11 past 3, 27 past 3 _____

   d. half past 4, quarter past 4, quarter to 4, half past 3 _____

2. Add two hours and 10 minutes to each of these digital times:

   a. 2:14 _____   **b.** 3:36 _____

   c. 8:08 _____   **d.** 10:41 _____

   e. 1:01 _____   **f.** 11:00 _____

   g. 4:45 _____   **h.** 7:15 _____

3. **a.** How many years in 2 centuries? _____

   b. How many days in April and January combined? _____

   c. If the last day of October is a Sunday, what day is the 1st of November? _____

   d. What is the day after December 31st, 1999? _____

4. Name 5 different timetables that are used in day-to-day living.

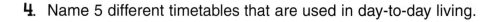

5. Name 3 instruments that are used to measure time.

   _____   _____   _____

6. Circle the greater time:

   a. 120 minutes or 3 hours   **b.** 30 seconds or ¾ minutes

   c. 600 days or 2 years   **d.** 2 decades or 2 centuries

   e. 24 hours or 1 ½ days   **f.** 7 months or 7 weeks

Name	**Date**

1. Nicholas II, the last Tsar of Russia ruled for 23 years. If he abdicated in 1917, what year did he begin his reign? _____

2. In 1980, Brazilian soccer player Edson Arantes do Nascimento was voted "Athlete of the Century". Which century is this and how many decades have passed since then? _____

3. In 1961 Alan Shepherd was the first American astronaut in space. A decade later, as leader of the Apollo 14, he planted the American flag on the moon. What year was this? _____

4. Beethoven moved to Vienna in 1792. Twenty-seven years later he was totally deaf. What year was this? _____

5. The first fleet arrived in Australia in 1788. Scientists believe that Aborigines had inhabited the land for more than 50,000 years. How many centuries is this? _____

6. Victor Hugo, a poet and novelist was born in 1802. He lived for 63 years. In what year did he die? _____

7. Homer, an ancient Greek poet, lived in the ninth century BCE. He wrote about the Trojan War and the city of Troy. After each war the city was rebuilt on top of the old one. It is believed that the seventh city was destroyed in 1200 BCE. How many centuries passed until Homer was born? _____

   Challenge: What does BCE mean? _____

8. In 1922 a British archaeologist found Tutankhamen's tomb in Egypt. Tutankhamen died in 1352 BCE. For how many years did his tomb go undiscovered? _____

9. Galileo, a mathematician and astronomer, was born in 1564. If he lived for 77 years, in what year did he die? _____

10. When Charles Dickens was 12 years old, he was sent to work in a London factory. If he started work in 1824, in what year was he born? _____

Name	**Date**

Everyone who lives in Oomdarby just loves eating marshmallows. One day when Marcy Mills was cleaning up she noticed that there was only one marshmallow left in her barrel. A very strange thing happened as she watched! Five minutes later there were two, and five minutes after that there were four. In fact the number doubled every five minutes. She was very excited.

1. How many marshmallows would there be after:

    a. 10 minutes? _____

    b. 25 minutes? _____

    c. half an hour? _____

    d. three quarters of an hour? _____

    e. 1 hour? _____

2. How long would it take for there to be 16,384 marshmallows? _____

Everyone kept their marshmallows in barrels which held 262,144 of them altogether.

3. How long would it take to fill:

    a. 1 barrel? _____

    b. half a barrel? _____

    c. 2 barrels? _____

4. Now make up two questions for a friend to answer.

    a. _____

    _____

    b. _____

    _____

Skills Index

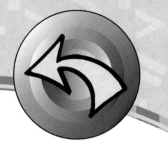

The following index lists specific objectives for the student pages of each unit in the book. The objectives are grouped according to the sections listed in the Table of Contents. Use the Skills Index as a resource for identifying the units and student pages you wish to use.

Length

Estimates, measures, and records the length of objects in inches. (Pages: 8, 11, 18, 28)

Represents, interprets, and explains mathematical technology including graphs and diagrams. (Page: 9)

Uses standard informal units. (Page: 9)

Measures perimeter.
(Pages: 10, 11, 20, 25, 27)

Uses available technology to help in the solution of mathematical problems. (Page: 11)

Uses number skills involving whole numbers to solve problems. (Pages: 16, 17, 18, 30)

Uses one or more strategies to solve mathematical problems. (Pages: 19, 29)

Poses questions or problems about mathematical situations. (Pages: 19, 29)

Directly and indirectly compares lengths. (Page: 20)

Checks, using an alternative method if necessary, whether answers to problems are correct and sensible. (Pages: 20, 27)

Makes conversions between measurement units. (Page: 25)

Counts, compares, orders, and calculates with decimals (up to two places). (Pages: 25, 26)

Selects and carries out the operation appropriate to situations involving addition and subtraction. (Page: 27)

Estimates, measures, and records length in miles. (Page: 30)

Area

Demonstrates an understanding of the concept of area. (Page: 35)

Can relate the concept of area to everyday situations. (Page: 35)

Measures and compares areas of shapes using informal units. (Page: 36)

Demonstrates an understanding of boundaries. (Page: 37)

Demonstrates an understanding of the relationship between the boundary of a shape and its area. (Page: 38)

Orders shapes according to area. (Page: 38)

Demonstrates an understanding of the concept of tessellations. (Page: 39)

Calculates area with a formal unit of measure.(Pages: 44, 45)

Demonstrates an understanding of a square foot. (Page: 46)

Records area by short method. (Page: 46)

Demonstrates an understanding of a square inch. (Page: 47)

Applies knowledge and understanding of area to problem solving. (Page: 48)

Mass

Approximates, counts, compares, orders, and represents whole numbers and groups to 100. (Page: 53)

Selects and carries out the operation appropriate to situations involving addition and subtraction. (Page: 54)

Uses understood written methods to add and subtract any whole numbers. (Page: 54)

Represents, interprets, and explains mathematical situations using everyday language with some mathematical terminology including graphs and diagrams. (Page: 54)

Uses number skills involving whole numbers to solve problems. (Pages: 55, 61, 62)

Estimates, compares, and records the mass of objects to the nearest pound and recognizes the need for a unit smaller than the pound. (Pages: 55, 63)

Compares and orders length, capacity, and mass in common standard units. (Page: 60)

Appreciates the impact of mathematical information on daily life. (Page: 61)

Measures and records the mass of objects to the nearest ounce. (Pages: 61, 63)

Uses one or more strategies to solve mathematical problems. (Page: 63)

111

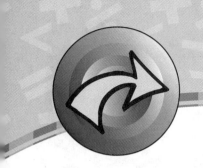

Skills Index

Capacity and Volume

Estimates, compares, and records the capacity of containers to the nearest gallon. (Page: 68)

Recognizes the need for units smaller than a gallon. (Page: 68)

Identifies and names the measurements that can be made for an object. (Pages: 69, 76, 78)

Records information about the capacity of a range of containers in a table and/or a graph. (Pages: 70, 77)

Estimates, compares, and orders the capacity of containers to the nearest liter. (Page: 75)

Recognizes the need for units smaller than a liter. (Page: 75)

Angles

Makes sensible estimates based on provided units. (Page: 83)

Identifies angles in turns. (Pages: 83, 87)

Uses indirect methods to order angles. (Pages: 84, 86)

Uses direct comparison to identify angles. (Page: 85)

Identifies and orders angles using direct comparison. (Pages: 85, 86)

Time

Understands the concept of o'clock and half past. (Page: 92)

Understands and demonstrates time in quarter hour intervals. (Page: 93)

Tells time on both analog and digital clocks. (Page: 94)

Reads and writes time in hours and minutes. (Pages: 95, 105)

Writes time in words and numerals. (Page: 96)

Demonstrates an awareness of time and seasons. (Pages: 97, 107)

Names and orders seasons and months. (Pages: 97, 107)

Orders time in hour and minute intervals. (Page: 102)

Demonstrates concept of A.M. and P.M. (Page: 103)

Uses a calendar to describe the day and date. (Page: 104)

Calculates time in minute intervals. (Page: 106)

#8992 Targeting Math: Measurement